GENTLE REPARENTING

The ORIGINAL guide
For therapists and clients

previously published as:
GET THE LOVE YOU
DESERVE How to Fill
Those Voids Within
and then
HEART TO HEART HEALING

by Jeannie Alvin, M.A.

I dedicate this to The Beloved,
and to all my healers.

ACKNOWLEDGEMENTS

Thanks to my healers,
and to all those who were kind to me.

ABOUT THE AUTHOR

The author, Jeannie Alvin, M.A., is uniquely qualified to write this. She lived through the discovery of this new type of healing as she healed, and then recognized that it was, in fact, a new path.

Jeannie had failed to heal for years in a number of healing methods, and had been told repeatedly that she was too damaged and was not healable. When she began to heal in only three 50-minute sessions a month, she knew that if she, as damaged as she was, could heal, a new door was opening for many others.

She later became a healing partner for others   to fill their voids.   She subsequently taught classes to practitioners, and documented their positive results a year later in her master's thesis. Her college papers, journals, and other

work were copywritten

in the Library of Congress beginning in 1980.

The author received a B.A.and an M.A.

in Psychology from Goddard College in

Plainfield, Vermont in 1983 and 1987,

respectively.

She then became a healing partner as a

counselor, then as a psychotherapist in Denver,

Colorado. She periodically offered classes

ranging from two to four hours to a weekend

seminar. She gained state accreditation to offer a

class to counselors who treated recovering

alcoholics.

She speaks fluent Spanish, and is learning French,
so that she can speak to many people about
healing in their own language.

TABLE OF CONTENTS

1

PROLOGUE

Famine Of The Heart, The Plague Of Our Times

We have a famine in our world as serious in its destructive force as the 1984 famine in Ethiopia. It is devastating the lives of rich and poor, old and young, educated and uneducated. Our famine is emotional starvation, observable through all walks of life. While emotional starvation does not cause all problems, it is the root cause of much of the misery that permeates our culture and our world.

The famine in Ethiopia left death. Emotional starvation in our homes, our schools, our businesses, our social programs, our local and national governments, leaves not only the dead, victims of drive-by shootings, gang warfare, drug abuse, suicide and other tragedies. It also leaves the living dead, from whom we avert our gaze. They may shuffle past us on the streets, beg for money in front of the grocery stores, or silently go about their work in our offices, avoiding our eyes. It is now so blatant that it is getting hard for even the most determined to ignore signs of this famine. It is a famine of the heart, the plague of our times.

My parents were affected by this famine. Their emotional starvation was the cause of my childhood abuse and misery. Much less emotional starvation than I endured can cause serious disruption in people's pursuit of happiness and well-being. Yet a wide range of people, from desperately miserable and dysfunctional as I had been, to healthy and functioning people, have benefitted from techniques and experiences similar to the ones that helped me.

Most people have at least an occasional sense of being trapped by life's circumstances. It may occur with the birth of a handicapped child, poverty, the loss of a loved one, or being in the wrong job. In a myriad of ways, life's circumstances can appear to be insurmountable. Carma Lord is a 49 year old woman who felt this way. She had just received the shattering knowledge that her difficulties in the past years were caused by multiple sclerosis. Her reaction to this event expresses poignantly how many of us feel when life seems to trap us.

Carma's beautiful poem speaks to our hearts. We all can identify some times when we have felt like we were trapped, with no way out.

MONARCH BUTTERFLY, by Carma Lord

I am a Monarch butterfly caught in a jar. I
flap and flap my wings, but I can't go far.

I beat myself to death trying to escape. I
am so filled with panic, anger, and hate.

I'm so tired and my wings are torn.

There is little air left and my spirit is
worn.

I had so many dreams and fields of flowers to
    explore.
I can't spread my wings anymore.

Can't someone see I'm not moving and I'm at
    the bottom of the glass.
Please open this jar fast!

I escaped the trap of the unhappy life that my abusive childhood had created.   My subsequent healing raises questions for politics and governments, therapies, social agencies, schools, jails, and most important, for child-rearing practices and child-rearing support systems. While healing emotional starvation will not solve all problems, it will solve some, and help many people.

My intention is that the lessons people learn from my struggles and solutions will help create personal change. With enough personal changes in our culture, political and social changes can occur. Perhaps then the famine of the heart plaguing our times will only be something our grandchildren read about in history books.

CHAPTER 1

Many Roads to Rome

Have you ever reached a crossroads in your life, where looking back, you did some things and experienced some things that changed your life forever?

Many people are searching for intimacy. Could many of the keys to intimacy be found in pre-schools? Can adults experience something so profoundly simple and have their lives work better? Will they have the courage to request and try it?

There is a golden thread of truth that runs through all religions, through the teachings of all of the great masters, through what is great and profound in education, in love, through whatever <u>really</u> works in all areas of our lives. This truth is often very simple and has great power. The experiences that healed me after I reached my crossroads were also very simple and powerful. They got me out of the trap of my life circumstances. They bring early childhood education out of the halls of academia and pre-schools, into psychology, education, churches and temples. I want to share my experiences with integrity. I know that my search for love and intimacy, and my discoveries, have something in common with all humans, and have the potential to help others.

The experiences that healed me were those seen in day-care homes and in pre-schools. The profound difficulty I had when I needed to eat, and chronic low energy were ameliorated in great degree by being held by a warm person and drinking from baby bottles. My inability to experience any degree of intimacy was healed by being held and being truly listened to by a person who allowed me to become dependent. The torturous events of my infancy and childhood were healed to some degree by my regained ability to feel the emotions associated with past events, after I had experienced enough support to be able to face them. I gained support for living through the days outside of the healing sessions with a new mental structure that I created from powerful statements from my healing partners.

Why doesn't our world work better? Sometimes it seems that most humans grow up in dysfunctional families. It is certainly true that most of us have voids, or holes, in the continuum of development that began at our birth, or even before. When we are over-stressed, or lose someone we love, we can fall into those holes and experience the worst pain of our lives. My holes and traumas were extreme, but pain is pain, and when we hurt, we all hurt in similar ways. We may behave in a variety of ways as we react to our pain. Still, the underlying pain that I feel when I hurt is the same pain that you feel when you hurt.

I may or may not have had more holes to fall into than you have, and fewer tools to dig myself out, yet on my path toward healing I discovered how to fill in those voids. I was told by numerous psychiatrists and psychologists that these voids could not be filled.

The doors for filling voids in a gentle and natural way were not opened until I discovered them, because the healing professions had no answers for me, nor for anyone else on a quest for filling in the voids. The psychiatrists and psychologists treat the <u>effects</u> and symptoms of those voids. I learned how to remove the <u>cause</u>.

I also learned many tools for alleviating the pain. The more I learned, the more connected I became to myself and other people, and to Spirit, to God, that higher power.

I was as emotionally unhealthy as a person can be and remain alive. I now have loving, close relationships. My friends tell me that I am a gift in their lives, as they are in mine. I take so naturally to the ability I now have to attract good people to me. I am able to read the signs of trouble, and usually stay away from mean or untrustworthy people.

My Crossroads, When My Healing Began

I reached my major crossroads in 1979. I was too miserable to continue in the direction I had been going. I was thirty-three years old, divorced, the single parent of a four year old, and deeply depressed. I wished I were dead, but I wouldn't kill myself because I knew my suicide would irreparably harm my son.

Sometimes a child becomes a great motivator for a parent. My son's needs spurred me on to try again to heal after each failure.

I was diagnosed as having zero prognosis for recovery, and for living. I did not believe those professional opinions, although in retrospect they were correct in terms of professional knowledge at that time, and for the most part, today as well.

This is a new path that has not yet reached most helping professionals. This is a path of healing the <u>cause</u>, rather than treating the <u>effects</u>, which are the symptoms. My belief that I could heal played an important role in my forging this new path and my consequent healing.

It was considered by professionals that I had no chance of healing. They gave my diagnosis labels, several syllable words, and usually a different one with each professional that I saw! The use of these labels caused me additional pain that I did not need. The new pain came because of the stigma, fear, and misunderstanding of these conditions in our culture. Also, the use of these labels towards me served professionals only enough for them to tell me that I was not healable.

The use of their diagnosis as a descriptor of me was dehumanizing. The use of these labels always coincided with a denial of me as a thinking person, as a partner in my own healing. The people labeling me in this way never included any acknowledgement that I was a highly intelligent person with dreams and ambitions, with gifts inside that I wanted to develop and give. Like everyone, I wanted to live a full life. Those who labeled me were also outspoken in their opinions that I had little future, little to give, and they certainly were not interested in my thoughts.

The beauty of the healing method described here is that people are diagnosed according to unmet needs. And there is no human that I have met without some unmet needs. The person is honored more this way, it seems to me.

Almost everyone experiences feelings of isolation. Almost everyone experiences the desire for more intimacy, to feel understood, to be acknowledged and accepted, to truly feel loved. In those intensely quiet and honest moments when you are reflecting deeply on your life, when you look back at where you have been, and forward to where you want to go, do you not long for more of these experiences? The longings that we feel at times like this are pointers to what is possible, and clues to missing building blocks.

Missing Building Blocks, Those Voids Within

Almost all adults have missed receiving at least a few building blocks of childhood on their path of development. With some simple methods of returning to that place on the pathway where something is missing, we can get our unmet needs satisfied, and fill in those missing building blocks, even if we are many years removed from childhood.

The people that we call mentally ill only have more missing building blocks and fewer or no tools to dig themselves out of holes than the average person. As for the chemical imbalances for which the mentally ill are treated, some of those imbalances are the result of emotional starvation. Those will be alleviated when the tremendous voids are filled in. If you check the chemical balance of the people in Ethiopia who are starving, and then check it again when they are fed regularly, I venture to say that their body chemistry would be awry when starving, and return to normal when not starving. There is a parallel. Many of the chronically mentally ill are emotionally starving. Missing building blocks of infancy, which the mentally ill usually are missing, are the building blocks of love and trust. <u>They are starving for infant love</u>. Many can be healed. The drugs with which many are treated can have serious long-term side effects, and only alleviate symptoms.

If you want an easy way to guess what the emotional age of a person is, look at their behavior and functioning. Ask yourself what age baby or child exhibits that behavior. The chronically mentally ill often have difficulty feeding themselves, bathing and grooming themselves, and maintaining the adult functions of creating a home and working. What age baby or child cannot feed or groom itself? A small infant cannot feed or take care of itself. Of course an infant cannot work or create a home. Do you know adults who have temper tantrums, and want everything their own way, and want what they want right now? Does this remind you of a toddler in the "terrible two's?"

Everyone, doctors and lawyers, bricklayers and waitresses, was once an infant. For many of us, much happened that interrupted the experiences of bonding, love, emotional, intellectual and spiritual development in infancy or later in childhood.

When we don't develop in these needed ways, a small inner part of us remains waiting, undeveloped, longing for these needs to be met. When the voids are small, the disruptions in a life that is fulfilling in love and work and contribution to others are minor. Yet a lack of intimacy may be the exorbitant price paid for that small missing building block. When the voids are great, the disruption in one or more of these major areas of our lives is also great. People who have difficulty functioning in the adult world of work, adult relationships, and contributing to others are likely to be suffering from large voids in the building blocks of their infant or childhood development.

Clues in Adults That Point to Missing Building Blocks in Infancy

There are clues in adults that indicate missing building blocks. If you discover that you are missing a building block, do not be overly concerned. You are only missing an experience that you can choose to recoup, even years after the original missing or traumatic experience.

Following are clues that indicate missing infant building blocks, those from the first six months to a year after birth, in adults:

1. Thinking back to your own childhood, did you feel loved? (Not
did you <u>know</u> it, but did you <u>feel</u> it?) Do you consider your mother to be a warm and loving person? Your father? Did you consider yourself close to them? If you answered no to any of these questions, you may be missing an important developmental building block from infancy. If you answer "yes" to the following questions, you may have a missing building block from infancy:
2. Do you have difficulties with food? Do you feel hunger as a signal in your stomach that you need to eat, or do you eat according to the clock? Do you get dizzy or have a headache, or eat for some reason other than a signal from your stomach? You do not feel a hunger signal in your stomach, and a stomach signal of fullness after eating.

3. Do you feel that you never receive enough love, money, or possessions?

4. Your viewpoint of the world is that people are not okay, or they cannot be trusted.

5. You do not like to be touched, you find yourself isolated, or a loner; affection is not a part of your life.

6. You cannot easily identify what you want and what you do not want.

7. You often need to be in control, dominate, "be right," and are very critical and judgmental.

8. You are unable to experience pleasant sensations in your genital areas, or are hypoglycemic, or are an extremely "hyper" person who never slows down. If you suffer from eating disorders, feel pressure instead of emotions, have suicidal or homicidal plans or thoughts, feel helpless and inadequate, and feel dependent or fight to avoid feelings of dependency, if you use anger to avoid feeling fear, if you deny your needs and wants, if you are unable to be close and intimate with others, if you are obese, if you are unable to participate in the normal world of work, if you have been in a mental hospital, or a jail cell, you probably have missing building blocks from infancy.

Guide for Healers and Seekers of Healing

How does a newborn baby experience love and how can adults re-create that experience? We <u>can</u> re-create the essential experiences for adults to recapture the unmet building blocks from infancy to adolescence. There are needs to be met in each of the six stages of infancy and childhood development from both a warm woman and a warm man. Anyone can miss receiving one or more of them in any stage. Clues that indicate missing building blocks in the stages of development beyond infancy will follow in other chapters of this book. Also, further chapters will explain how to fill the voids in adults from all of the ages and stages of childhood.

I don't know if I should classify what happened as I healed an educational experience, a therapy, a love experience, or a spiritual awakening. Carl Jung, one of the great masters of psychology, stated that every psychological problem is ultimately a matter of religion. In his book, <u>Care of the Soul</u>, Thomas Moore takes what he calls the Renaissance approach of not separating psychology from religion. In this book, I do not separate psychology, spirituality, or education. There are many educational and personal growth courses, and the experiences I had could conceivably fit the parameters that define these courses. And there are a myriad of ways that people find love. Before these experiences, I did not believe in God, although I remember wishing that I could at least have had that comfort. These

14

experiences were a very unusual way to find love, but they worked for me. As I discovered love, in my own way, I found myself to be loved by God, and had some meaningful spiritual experiences. I've heard the old saying, "There are many roads to Rome." This was my road. Perhaps it will be yours. I've struggled for years with the question of how to label the experiences that changed my life from utter and complete misery to feeling good most of the time. So I will simply describe the healing and growth-enhancing experiences and the results.

After eight fruitless years of trying various therapies and healing methods, I finally found myself beginning to heal! As I began to heal, I was given two gifts at once.

I began, at last, to feel good sometimes and to connect to people for the first time in my life. That was gift number one. And simultaneously, I experienced a second gift.

As I made these gains, I <u>knew</u>, in the deepest part of myself, what aspects of the experiences could be meaningful and helpful to others. These impressions turned out to be true; they were to prove helpful to others. This knowing is sometimes called intuition or inner knowing.

I kept a journal, which I called "Coming Alive." Nine months after I began to heal, my healing partner asked me to join him in offering this to others, with favorable, sometimes dramatic results.

I later taught a short version of these important experiences to other facilitators. They were able to add aspects of this type of healing to their work.

People read the college paper I wrote in 1983 for my B.A. at Goddard College, in Plainfield, Vermont. In it I described this work, and compared it point by point with the harsh but similar process originating with Jacqui Schiff, who wrote <u>All My Children</u>, (a book, not the TV show!) Some wrote to me that they were inspired to try it after reading my college paper. I learned that other healers simply read my college paper and changed their therapy practice.

From experiencing and "knowing" that this was a repeatable path for others, I proved scientifically that it is. First I offered it to others, and documented the positive results in a college paper. Then I taught it to other healers, who were able to achieve positive results without my presence in the healing sessions. That is documented in college papers, as well.

So I decided to write my experiences in as clear a way as possible, knowing that many professionals will be able to simply read this material and begin to offer it to clients. Other people, in need of healing like I was, will be able to use this book as a guide in requesting healing experiences from people untrained in this new path. I believe that many, from the emotionally healthy, to those people like me, with glaring gaps in emotional health, will find it to be their own "Road to Rome."

My Life Prior To Healing

I will briefly discuss my own life prior to my crossroad experience, so that the reader has some idea of the long road I traveled, and how very much I was helped. My point with sharing my story is to show that anyone, no matter what the damage, can heal.

I sometimes forget that my life was almost the complete opposite of what it is now. As nice as I tried to be, no one used to like me. Few treated me well. I found mostly abusive people with whom to relate, people who would hurt me more. Physically I was toothpick thin, stiff and rigid. My movements were stiff and awkward. My voice was flat, like a computer verbalization. I looked like the "walking dead" that I nearly was. I was horrendously lonely and life was more painful than I could stand.

From the small glimpse of my childhood that I share in the next few pages, you may be able to sense the misery, hopelessness, joylessness and lovelessness that was my life for thirty-three years. You may see how the relatively simple experiences that will be described later in this book could be so important to someone having such a background. You may also see why such a background left tremendous voids.

To go from a life of hell to a real life is possible. Also, for you to go from a good life to a great life is possible. Perhaps you are one of the loving people who will give an hour or two of your

17

week to someone whose needs are as great as mine
were. You will then give someone else a life worth
living, and help reverse the tragedy of our times, this
famine of the heart.

My story is a very happy ending to a tragic
story. It is one of triumph over very difficult odds.
This could not have happened without the grace of
a few loving people who opened their hearts and
arms and ears to me in love and sympathy.

I've been asked how I can remember
incidents from early childhood and infancy. Some
were related to me by relatives, neighbors, and
family friends. Others surfaced in cathartic
emotional release sessions, years after healing began,
when I was finally able to begin facing the hurts
perpetrated on my body, and begin to tolerate the
feelings of pain and hurt, terror and rage.
Sometimes I experienced intense feelings in the
healing sessions. Impressions of what happened
would surface. I also had revealing dreams. I've
grown to believe that we contain a record of
everything that has happened to us in our mind and
bodies

.

Readers who wish to skip the stories of the
torture and abuse that I suffered may omit the
indented sections describing them. If you are very
sensitive, or for any reason wish not to read
descriptions of profound pain and suffering, I
suggest that you skip ahead beyond the indented
sections to the regular paragraphs.

Gentle Reparenting   The ORIGINAL Guide   J. Alvin

18

Before beginning to heal, I remembered nothing of my childhood except being kicked out of the house at age seventeen. As I began to heal, I remembered these events gradually as the amnesia about my whole childhood began to lift.

I was an honor student, always at the top of my classes. Because I was one of the top twelve juniors in our class rank, I was awarded the distinction of "Junior Escort."

I was attending the practice session for my part in the seniors' graduation ceremony. When I arrived home from school that day I found all my belongings scattered on the front lawn, and was locked out.

There had been no threats of such a dire consequence, although with my sister away at college, I had found it increasingly difficult to avoid my mother. Our contact, never good, had deteriorated.

I became suicidal that day, but decided to wait to kill myself until I was twenty-one. I thought I should be grown up to make such a large decision. The thought that I should be dead would not leave my mind until I reached that crossroads at age thirty-three.

The constant thoughts of suicide left me drained of energy. I now unconsciously feared success as the success of my junior escort experience became associated for me with becoming homeless and losing all my important   relationships and my belongings. I already feared almost everything about myself and others, and now feared success.

My parents told me many details about my infancy. They did so casually and sometimes proudly. They had solved a problem for themselves. They seemed to have no idea of the traumas they inflicted on me. They were young, immature, very ill-equipped even to deal with each other, much less a brood of children. They had children in a time before psychotherapy was readily available to people, and before it became a popular subject in the culture, as it has during the last fifteen years or so in the United States.

For as long as I can remember, my mother and father were at war with each other. There were daily screaming battles, every time my father arrived home. I would wait in dread, hoping that violence would not occur. My father is a cold, emotionless, domineering man, sneering when challenged, with a nccd to totally control. IIe is also highly intelligent, ambitious, and charming when things go his way. He always is certain that he alone is right, with a complacent assumption of his superiority over others. He berates most normal and natural desires and all emotional expression as "irrational."

Gentle Reparenting   The ORIGINAL Guide   J. Alvin

My mother is emotional to an extreme, often during my childhood, out of control. She attempts to totally control others by her emotional outbursts. She is also very intelligent, energetic, ambitious, and charming when she gets what she wants.

Both of my parents are college graduates, professionals. Many parents consciensciously do the best that they can. My parents both were too self-centered to think of anyone but themselves. Both my father and mother were pampered children of very dysfunctional families. Both expected to get their way, due to a childhood where their needs and demands were fulfilled without regard for other people's needs. In addition, they did not realize that they had almost nothing to give emotionally, and unknowingly passed their unresolved pain on to their children. I believe in the combination that they created together, these two people were worse parents than either might have been alone or with another partner. The abusive discipline they used was to get me to start or stop doing something. They apparently gave little or no thought to the effects on me of their harshness.

They both left great gaps of neglect and deprivation when they were not disciplining. My parents' acts of abuse were quickly forgotten by these two young people in their twenties, who had no adequate tools for childrearing, lack of emotional support, and financial difficulties. Unfortunately the result to me was a shutting down and closing off of everything about myself other than my mind.

However,it is important to show a more complete picture of them than abusive parents. Those harsh acts were, for them, a few moments in a few years of their lives. They have also done many kind, generous and fine things and have many accomplishments. From my earliest memories, both parents acknowledged my intelligence and potential. They enrolled me in childhood programs such as the Girl Scouts and many others, which greatly enhanced my learning as a child. I am glad that they each have found happiness with other partners in their old age.

As a newborn baby, I was my father's special baby. To help me be strong in life and to fight dangerous emotions, he instructed my mother not to go to me when I cried. She was to play the radio or turn on the vacuum cleaner, and only go to me when I became quiet. This certainly destroyed any opportunity for bonding that might have begun between my mother and me.

After years and years of healing, when I could tolerate the feelings, I experienced the pain of starving as a newborn. It felt like snakes biting me on the inside. Later, my grandmother told me that when she visited our house, when I was an infant, she often found me naked,lying in my own puddles on a cold wooden floor. My mother didn't want to bother with diapers.

Another memory surfaced from this time. I was sexually stimulated, and then fingers were inserted into me. The memory of great pain in that area returned in my healing. I have the uncomfortable conscious memory of my mother's odd comment to me, "You were a hot baby!"

At approximately nine months to a year old, when I could toddle around, I began to scream regularly when my father left for work. I tried to catch him to keep myself safe. When he left, I was burned by cigarettes and bitten by my   mother, in addition to being starved.

More training on fighting those dangerous feelings was to come! My parents prepared a tub of cold water, and had it waiting. When I   screamed for my daddy, he returned. They picked me up and dunked me under the cold water. They pushed me back under every time I came up screaming. I finally came up quiet, unconscious. I thought my parents were killing me. My mother told me that my voice immediately changed that day, from a high-pitched one to a low one.

This has been a very difficult trauma to recuperate from in my healing. I have only recovered in part. In many sessions I remembered bits and pieces of the trauma, and little by little experienced the life-threatening terror that was too much for a baby to feel.

The memories of being burned and bitten surfaced in therapy. The words, "Don't burn me, don't bite me," came out of my mouth, again and again, with tears, and me screaming "No,no!" And again, "Don't burn me, don't bite me."

After several sessions like this, I told my therapist that I knew my mother was disturbed, but I had a hard time believing that she would burn me, although I remembered her biting my younger brothers, to teach them not to bite each other. That very week, a relative confided that Mom had confessed, "Don't tell anyone, I regret this, but when the girls were little I'd get so angry I'd bite them."

Obviously both she and my father were very disturbed emotionally to have done these things and the other cruel acts that punctuated a long and joyless childhood, culminating with a total abdication of parental responsibility when my

24

mother kicked me out of the house at age seventeen.
What was done to them in their infancy and early
childhood, to perhaps pass on cruel acts from which
they hadn't healed? And perhaps even more to the
point, what wasn't done for them in their infancies
and childhood years? What were their voids? What
parenting was missing, or what was done to my
mother to create a human who could act in such
uncontrolled frenzy? What was done, and what was
missing, for my father to be so totally emotionless
and insensitive that he could design acts of
starvation and drowning, and perpetrate them upon
an infant?

At age four and a half I stopped
talking. I could only whisper. This resulted
from being given an enema with an adult-
sized quantity of water. I remember how it
began. First I was put on the kitchen table,
lying on my back. Then the table leaf on
the side was put up, squeezing my arm in
horrible pain. Then I was held still while too
much water was forced into me. Now every
part of my body had been invaded.

After that I could only whisper. This
old reaction continues to appear on those
now rare occasions that I am over-stressed.
In those times I whispered or cannot talk.

I also remember at about age five, my
father saying, as he waited to "gain self-
control" before spanking, that he

spanked me on my thighs as he had learned that he wouldn't break my legs by hitting me there. While he waited to gain his self-control, he held me over his knees with my panties down. I waited in terror for him to hit, as he droned on about how great he was to have such control.

At this same age, I remember when my parents daily war became violent. My daily fear was of this sort of ferocity surfacing in their daily screaming and belittling matches. This day my sister and I were huddled at the end of the kitchen counter in terror. We were unable to escape as we would have had to cross the battle zone. My dear sister, only about six years old herself, tried to protect me as best she could. My parents were throwing dishes at each other and breaking everything. When they stopped, even their eyeglasses were broken. A while after the battle, I remember sitting on my father's lap, and hearing intense silence, and pointed out the pretty bubbles floating by. I escaped the feelings of terror that I could not tolerate by hallucinating.

The rest of my childhood was interspersed with abuse. I had so little sense of self that I was seven years old before I said "I" to refer to myself. School and learning became a safe and rewarding haven for me. I always learned very quickly and read voraciously. In high school I took the PSAT tests, and scored in the 99th percentile in most areas.

I covered the bruises on my upper thighs from the girls in my gym class, having a great fear of crying if anyone noticed. The bruises were from one hard slap of my father's hand. At first welts raised up around the edges of his finger marks, and a purple bruise in the shape of his hand appeared. These bruises took about three weeks to completely disappear, turning from an initial dark purple to yellow as they faded.

My Life After Some Healing; Forgiving

Before healing, I hated and feared my parents, and hid my whereabouts from them. After years of healing I forgave my parents, as I realized that I had received more love and understanding and tenderness in my healing than my poor parents may have received in their whole lives. Having been asked how I could forgive my parents, I looked back at myself prior to any healing. I, better than anyone I have met, know what it is like being so incapable of expressing the love I felt for my son, due to my severe blocking of my emotions. I remember that I loved him just the same, but I also ached because I could see how my mistakes and inabilities in expressing love were hurting my son. And I certainly knew how it felt to hurt.

I spoke to my dad twice about these horrendous incidents. I told him that just the one incident in the bathtub had cost me many years of relationships with people, because I was afraid of everyone.

That and other incidents had cost me at least twenty years of my adult life, as every spare penny went for therapy. It cost me the time and money that other people spend on the normal material pleasures of our culture. A nice car, a house, vacations, nice clothes, spending money, all were beyond my reach. All my spare financial resources went for healing.

I was committed that I would not pass on a loveless, friendless, joyless and hopeless life to my son. Thank God I succeeded. We both now have love, friends, joy and hope in our lives, although we both still have many shortcomings due to my history.

My father was very sad when I told him this. He was then in his late sixties, I in my late forties. We finally spoke to each other and felt close. We shared our feelings of love. He had initiated this conversation by saying that he had been scared to death of his father. He said that he hoped he hadn't been that way for his children. I told him that unfortunately we had been scared to death of him, and mentioned how the bathtub incident had crippled me emotionally, for all these years. In a broken voice he whispered that he was sorry. We spoke a second time of these sad acts. Then he said that this was too painful a subject for him to discuss further. He said he had done the best he could. I said I knew he had. By this time I fully realized how little my parents had to give emotionally, and the sad fact that the very little they gave me was truly all they had to give. They weren't intentionally withholding any emotional gifts.

Compassion

By this time I realized how little my parents had received emotionally from their own upbringing. I had some compassion for them, as I know how difficult it can be to go through life with so few internal resources.

A number of years after my healing sessions, I now felt good most of the time. So I decided to give my parents my unconditional love as a gift. I actually relate more to my mother now than to my father, but I see them both, and we share our love. Now that I don't need my mother to give me anything, she has been extremely generous to me. I very much appreciate her gifts as acknowledgement of the love that has grown between us. I thank God that they are still living, and that we have gotten to this point in our relationships while they are still alive.

My son is now twenty-one, a young man. I succeeded in my goal to have the family lineage of abuse stop with me. He is a warm, loving, easy-going person. His sixth grade teacher said he was the warmest person she had ever met. That's pretty great, considering that until he was four, he had a totally cold mother. As I got warmth from my healing partners, he got it from me. His opinion of his childhood is that it was fine, and he wouldn't change a thing. When I point out glaring gaps in areas where I lacked the tools and the emotional building blocks to meet his needs, he is very pragmatic, and says he's fine. He says that I couldn't help what I didn't have. He has a very generous heart. He continues to be a gift in my life.

By now you realize how much I had been hurt. I have healed, and am still healing, not perfectly, and not from everything. Healing will be ongoing with me for my whole life. Since life keeps getting better as I heal, and I know how, why stop?

My father didn't realize why he thought it was so important to teach me not to cry. But his mother, my grandmother, confided in me that as a tiny infant he was smothered with a pillow by his father who tried to stop his crying. In addition, perhaps tragedies that are too painful for people to deal with emotionally are passed on unconsciously to children. The tragedies on my father's side of the family were one sudden death by drowning, and another death by being horribly, accidentally burned.

On my mother's side, one tragedy was a grandmother being placed in an orphanage as a child, where she went hungry. She went searching for food in garbage cans. She was bitten by dogs and rats competing for the same food scraps.

My major childhood traumas involved hunger, bites, burns, and almost drowning, reflections of those family tragedies. Is this coincidence? Or do we need to have more compassion and offer more support to victims of tragedies? Our culture is not concerned with offering much emotional support. Do we not tend to blame victims, rather than offering support?

Notice our culture's attitude toward the homeless, many of them obvious victims of lack of the building blocks of childhood.

After reading this, you may feel blame and anger towards my parents for the hurts they inflicted on me. I certainly did until I had healed enough to let it go. But can you also see that they had been hurt? Can you also feel compassion for them, knowing that they've lived to an old age with unhealed traumas and great unfulfilled voids? And in spite of the fragility caused by the emotional wounds and great voids that she carries, my mother has the courage to bless my sharing of some of her darkest moments so that others can heal. Would you have her courage?

My hope is that you will be able to see possibilities for healing other hurt people, yourself included. I hope that you will also learn compassion for people who hurt people. I heard many people's life histories during a long internship. I learned that people who warped themselves always did so in order to survive when they were children. We all unconsciously leave a trail of hurt people behind. I have hurt people. You have hurt people. We have hurt the ones we love and those we don't love. We've hurt our friends. We've hurt our co-workers. We've hurt strangers. If we could look back on our path and see who we've hurt, each one of us, you and I, would see a trail of hurt bodies, minds and spirits, going back into the far distance. So let us not judge others. There's a very wise old Indian saying that before we judge, we should walk in the other person's moccasins. If you can begin to suspend your judgement of others, knowing that there are reasons beyond your awareness for their actions, that in itself will be a great step in growth for you.

Prior to some filling of the tremendous voids within me, I was unable to benefit from therapies, personal growth courses, or religion. After some of the voids had been partially filled, I was able to learn and grow from all of those.

It's Not Too Late To Have A Great Childhood

One of the gifts of the lovely healing experiences I had is that I no longer consider myself to have had an unhappy childhood. Yes, I had those awful experiences, then had the wonder and beauty of a very happy childhood starting at age thirty-three!

Some answers will be found within these pages for people committed to making a difference for the chronically mentally ill. What about alcoholics, drug addicts, and incest victims? Since holes can be filled in, it may take people with more holes longer to do the job, but it is possible. When many healthy people offer this type of healing, there will be many creative variations of this new path. Then our world can better heal the famine of the heart suffered by our needy people in such great numbers.

I am sharing my experiences to teach the possibilities of this new way of healing for people committed to giving to others, and for those in need of healing. I hope to inspire you to believe, in spite of whatever obstacles you have to overcome, that you can succeed in reaching your goals of healing or offering healing. I want to offer the gifts I was given to others, and to illustrate the power and the simplicity of these experiences.

Missing Building Blocks In Our Culture

There appears to be a need for healing in many of our professions. Some people in our culture who need help are not receiving it because of a lack of money. Money is an exchange of energy. Let's make it a fair exchange.

In the old days, farmers used to pay a doctor what they could, often a basket of vegetables and a chicken. Today, sometimes medical treatment costs the whole farm!

This greed bespeaks of an unhealthy area in the psyche of some people, a missing building block from infancy, that there is never enough money, love, possessions. More money, more zeroes in the bank account, another degree, another car will not fill those voids within.

Many people are not like this. In the obituary section was a lovely tribute to Dr. Arnold A. Ariaudo, a dentist for 60 years. When he began his dental career in 1934, he studied Spanish in order to better serve the farm workers. These workers were on the lowest rung of the economic ladder. He charged them on a sliding scale, taking only what they could afford. Sometimes that was lettuce, melons, potatoes or rhubarb.

The healers I now work with to complete my healing are treating me free of cost. They will continue to work with me until I am fully healed. They will not stop working with me for any reason. I believe this to be a spiritual reward for my lifelong commitment to healing, and the tremendous efforts I put forth to be healed.

A spiritual aspect of trade and commerce is that it is another opportunity for us to learn to give and receive, equitably and fairly. With a desire to fully experience giving and receiving, we can learn to give as we receive, by our attitude and sincere appreciation of gifts we are given. We can also learn to receive as we give, experiencing the pleasure of giving, and seeing the benefits that our gifts offer another person. When we have plenty, it is time to share. When we need, it is time to accept.

My childhood was truly a horror. But an even greater horror lies beyond my personal trials and misfortunes, or those of any one person. It is the horror stories and the missing building blocks that caused them, that lie like a gaping collective wound at the core of the famine of the heart in our culture.

If someone were to interview all of the people who have been suicidal, people who have been in mental hospitals or who are in jail cells, we would discover that a great percentage of these people have equally horrid childhood histories, with many missing building blocks of childhood.

Of those who don't have a childhood history of horror, how many have a history of absent parenting? How many people basically had to raise themselves? If this survey were done, many people would begin to get a sense, as I have, of understanding with compassion, although not condoning the wrong actions of these people.

I understand that it is hard to function in the adult world when childhood building blocks and tools for problem-solving are missing. Can you see that the more a person is missing, the harder it is for them to function?

As time goes by, I hope that more and more people gain understanding with compassion. When many decide to commit time, love, emotional support, understanding, and the filling of voids to as many people as possible, we will be able to reverse the famine of the heart that is the plague of our time.

We can only end a famine of the heart by a giving of the heart, and from the heart, many times over. We must reach the point of being able to give just because it is needed, as a service, and not for any other reward than the satisfaction of giving.

Bibliography and Resources:

All My Children, by Jacqui Lee Schiff, c. 1970, Jove Publications, Inc. NY.
The story of Jacqui Lee Schiff's discovery of the hungry baby inside young schizophrenic people.

Care of the Soul, by Thomas Moore, c. 1992, HarperCollins Publishers, NY,NY. A glimpse of the depth and sacredness in our everyday lives.

Chapter 2

My Healing Begins!

Perhaps you realize that you may have a few voids of your own that you could fill. So now I'll share with you a glimpse of how I began to fill my voids and began to heal. In the succeeding chapters I will include clues in adults to help you pinpoint areas of potential voids and potential growth in the remaining five stages of infancy and childhood. I will also detail how adults can fill any voids in the six stages of infant and childhood development. In addition, I will point out clues to voids in children.

The ages and stages of childhood have been observed and described by psychologists from Freud to Piaget to Erick Berne. Each stage has its own needs, and a child in each stage differs in his perception of himself and the world. This is the reason why adults with voids in the various stages of childhood have different viewpoints of reality. A person with voids in infancy will see an unsafe world, full of hurtful people who cannot be trusted. A person with early needs filled will see the same world as safe, and easily find trustworthy people with whom to relate.

The needs for parenting children varies in each of the six ages and stages of childhood. So naturally, filling those unmet needs in adults returning to those different ages and stages will vary according to the age and stage being addressed. Love needs vary with each stage. Love to a baby may be the timely response to a cry, being fed while being tenderly held in warm arms, and bonding very closely. In another stage the need may be for exploration. In one stage the need may be for totally positive, nonjudgemental attention, while in another the need may be for some correcting of behavior. Getting the love you deserve will vary in content and form as adults, as well as children, grow and heal.

I realized that my childhood and infancy needs were grossly unsatisfied. I became aware that the satisfaction of those needs would lead me to a life with love and easier and more successful functioning in the world.

Jacqui Lee Schiff's discovery of a "hungry baby" inside of her schizophrenic clients, and her decision to give these people a second chance for a healthy childhood, opened the door to healing severe problems. However, in her efforts to heal, she mistakenly believed that the way for hurt people to open was to use pain as a tool to break their defenses. (I discovered, to the contrary, that defenses come down when the environment is safe enough.) Her harsh treatment methods alongside of offering baby bottles and other childhood experiences appealed to few psychologists or clients, and only healed a few people. However, she is the true pioneer of this style of healing. It is indisputably her discovery. The gentleness and powerful statements that I discovered are more effective. These are important and needed changes in the atmosphere and treatment, but Jacqui Lee Schiff correctly discovered the needy infant inside of the chronically mentally ill. She provided a starting point for developing a treatment offering repeatable, easily teachable healing when none existed before.

I had great gaps in my early needs. Many readers will not have these great gaps. Not everyone will need to be fed a baby bottle, as I needed. Some will have later childhood needs. Those people will need to play and ask questions. Some people will have voids in adolescence. Their needs will reflect the sophistication of the almost grown child. The clues that point to later childhood and adolescent needs are described in chapter five.

It was not easy to find someone to hold me and feed me a baby bottle. Psychologists and psychiatrists are trained not to touch clients and to avoid letting clients get dependent on them. But if I were to have a healthy return to "infancy" as an adult, that meant that I would need to be dependent. It took all my courage to ask people to hold me and feed me a baby bottle. It was not easy to ask. I feared ridicule, and was very embarrassed to reveal this need.

I met a man whose eyes and quiet voice and manner appealed to me. He was a "counselor," lacking the formal training of psychologists and psychiatrists. I will call him Sam, not his real name. Fortunately for me, Sam hadn't been strictly trained not to touch clients. He offered me a gentle form of "bodywork," using breathing exercises to free emotional blocks. Sam was also highly trained in emotional release work, which he said I might use at some point in the future. We agreed to meet three times a month for fifty minutes.

In the sessions, Sam had me lie down on a foam mattress and do some gentle breathing exercises. After a few minutes of this breathing work, during which my body began to tingle, I would sit up and talk about my life. Sam would simply listen to me.

This was an enormous change from the psychologists I had consulted before. For the first time, I experienced being listened to non-judgementally, being <u>truly</u> heard. I asked about the strange sensations that occurred during our breathing work. Sam said softly, "You are coming alive."

I told Sam of my harsh childhood, followed by the harsh therapy I pursued fruitlessly for eight years. I told him of those professionals' belief that pain, in the form of harsh verbal confrontations and long hours standing in a corner, would "break" my defenses. Sam said that he believed that gentleness was the key to my treatment.

Gentleness! The proponents of the harsh and confrontational treatment I had undergone told me that gentle methods had been tried and failed; that people like me were not helped by comfort.

I told Sam that I needed him to feed me baby bottles, and to be held in his arms like a baby. I told him of the great dependency that could develop. I don't remember if I told him about the possibility that I would regress into childhood, then grow up again with him providing the parenting. I knew that most of the healing was simply having a good infancy and childhood in a bond with new parent figures.

Sam had never heard of such treatment! Throughout his years of counseling, other clients had expressed yearnings to be held and fed, but no one had asked him for the actual experience until I did. He decided to venture into the unknown with me, and complied with many of my requests, if they "felt right" to him. Although asking for what I believed I needed was very hard at first, Sam was so kind that asking became easy! I soon progressed to demanding!

Sam agreed to continue seeing me three times a month for fifty minutes, hold me, feed me baby bottles, and continue the rest of the session as before, with breathing exercises and talking. Later, our contact expanded to include a brief phone call each evening. I kept a journal of my progress, which I called, "Coming Alive." Excerpts from my journal are in the appendix.

People who have fewer voids than I had are able to spend an hour or two a week in healing sessions acting as if they were very small children, then go on with the rest of their week and their lives as if they had just spent an hour or two with a friend. This type of healing experience causes no disruption in their lives, their unmet childhood needs get fulfilled, and their relationships and functioning improve.

But people whose early needs were grossly unsatisfied may regress almost completely, as I did. They will then very naturally progress from stage to stage until they are "grown up" again, this time healthier. I knew I was a thirty-three year old woman, but I also knew that I was a four and a half year old child! The woman faded into the background, and the child dominated my personality. Fortunately Sam had been a pre-school teacher before becoming a counselor! He had some years of practice using gentle methods to handle child-like behavior!

My friends were horrified at the changes in me! I had turned from a quiet, withdrawn, intelligent computer programmer into a sometimes loud woman who played at the beach all day. I was evicted from a restaurant for singing at the top of my lungs, off key, in the ladies' room. I had come in off of the beach to use their restroom.

My friends may have been horrified, but I knew I was healing! From the theories expressed in the eight years of harsh therapy I had undergone, I knew that most of what I needed to heal was for me to have the infancy and childhood that I was denied with my parents. I experienced "being a baby" in my three counseling sessions a month, and at home, where I fixed my own baby bottles. The rest of the time I played as a small child plays, for the first time in my life. I sent my son to be cared for by others, as I could not take care of him while I was regressed.

After a few weeks of sessions with Sam, I had a revelation. I realized that if the harsh but pioneering treatment could heal a few people, then these gentle experiences obviously were heralding a new treatment for many people. I was one of the most severely damaged clients to attend the Jacqui Schiff treatment, with the worst eating difficulties that she had ever seen. I had attended her treatment full time, but I did not heal. In fact, I left more damaged than when I arrived. If I could begin to heal in only three fifty-minute sessions a month, the door to the healing possibilities suddenly seemed to open wide. I had discovered a successful gentle version that the pioneers and practitioners of this type of treatment were sure didn't exist! Some of those very pioneers were quick to quietly adopt my gentler version after reading my college paper.

After nine months of healing sessions, of massive doses of comfort and wonderful listening, and attentive parenting from this loving man, my eating difficulties were greatly relieved. I felt good for the first time in my life, and was able to tolerate being angry, scared, and sad for short periods. Prior to this time, I thought "feeling good" was when no one was hurting me. I was beginning to connect with people in a way I never had before.

I shared my discovery of the gentle method of treatment with people who were familiar with Jacqui Schiff's "children." I visited the Eric Berne Seminar

in San Francisco while I was still "a child," in 1979.
I was thrilled to meet notables there such as Steve
Karpman, who had defined the "drama triangle" of
rescuer,persecutor, victim; and others who had been
members of the seminar since the days when Eric
Berne, the founder of the seminar, was alive. I was
made a lifetime honorary member of the seminar.

Healing Other People Begins

After these initial nine months of a childhood, I
"grew up" and became a co-counselor with Sam. He
was intrigued by my progress in healing, and wanted
my help in offering it to others.

During a long internship, Sam and I offered
these experiences to clients in once-per-week
sessions at a large clinic, with very good results.

Some of the most poignant memories of that
time involve children. My son was six years old.
We lived with a man, and my son asked him to be
his daddy. The man opened his arms, and gathered
my son into a hug. They bonded closely, and my
son soaked up love and trust from him. Also, I now
was able to give my son warmth. One day he
playfully cried like a little baby, and said, "Waah,
waah, I'm your angel baby." This brought tears to
my eyes and goosebumps. During the first six
weeks of his life I had called him angel baby. After
that I had used another affectionate nickname. It

was a clue to me that he was remembering and healing the voids of his infancy.

One male client was so rigid and stiff in his movements that the other clients called him "the puppet." Although very handsome, he was very stiff and mechanical. He occasionally brought his small three-year-old son along with him. Sam and I saw him for a year, doing the breathing exercises, holding him and offering a baby bottle, and listening to him. Then he joined a therapy group conducted by a doctor at the center.

A year later the doctor shared a letter from this client with us. He wrote that his little boy, now five years old, said, "When I was little, you couldn't take care of me. Go to the store and buy me some baby bottles and take care of me now." So he went to the store, bought some baby bottles, and let his son "be a baby."

This points to new possibilities for treating children. I once read of a foster home for difficult pre-school children. In the basement was a rocking chair, baby toys, and cribs. The children were told that they could go down there and "be a baby again" if they wanted to. Then they were held and cared for by a warm person. At first they avoided the basement, but eventually all were drawn to it. They were "babies again" as long as they wanted to be. All of the children benefitted, were no longer "difficult children," and adjusted well to new foster homes.   I hope that the awareness that people get from reading this book creates a grass roots demand for people to get their baby and childhood needs satisfied. I hope that it gets easier to find people who will hold other adults and offer a baby bottle, warmth, unconditional listening, and other needs of childhood.

In the future I would totally regress to childhood two more times, each time taking a leap forward in healing. My personal relationships improved afterwards, although they suffered during each time I was regressed. My ability to function in the world around me was substantially less during the periods of regression, then improved greatly each time I "grew up."

I now have the skeletal structure of a healthy framework from which I relate to others, and enjoy my life. The damage from the severe abuse is so great that I will continue to heal my whole life. I still have some difficulties that impede me at times. I don't balance my energy well. I internally push myself, and seem unable to truly rest. When I attempt to work a normal eight-hour day, I collapse after two to three months. I still am not in a close relationship with a man. I have done more healing work regarding my mother than my father, and have more close relationships with women than with men.

Because of the magnitude and volume of the torturous and abusive acts perpetrated upon me, in addition to the glaring gaps in my emotional development, my progress towards complete healing is slower than that of most people. Once I typed a simple list of the abuse chronologically, with no details or story. The list went on for 18 pages, typed, double spaced. The abusive incidents that I shared in the previous chapter were only to give a glimpse of the damage I suffered, so that there is knowledge that all damage can potentially be healed.

I was fortunate because the first and most frequent feeling that I began to experience as I healed was feeling good and being able to receive love and warmth from others. Very gradually, I began to experience the emotions concerning the abusive incidents. Still later, I was able to express words and emotions towards pillows representing my parents in healing sessions. I grew in health and strength as I progressed, and as I continue to progress.

In the first weeks and months of my regression to childhood with Sam, I wanted to shout this good news from the rooftops, so that others like me could begin to heal. I realized that I needed to gain credentials in the field of psychology so that people in the healing professions would listen to me. I learned that this type of healing had to show its effectiveness without my presence.

I overcame many of the fears that stopped me from pursuing higher education. In 1983, in two quarters, I completed the two years I needed for my B.A. in Psychology from Goddard College in Plainfield, Vermont. I graduated on my thirty-seventh birthday. Two years later I graduated from

Goddard with an M.A. By the time I had my B.A. and M.A. in Psychology, I had shown that this treatment worked without my presence, in the treatment settings of other healers. Besides earning my credentials, I had the satisfaction of knowing that my discoveries were proven and documented.

I taught other facilitators a short course in the basics. The basics include a healer who has the building blocks of love and trust, at a minimum; the advanced listening skills needed to create a loving, responsive atmosphere; knowledge of certain powerful statements that can help create a new mental structure; how to respond to needs in different stages; and skills in emotional release work. (The basics are in chapters three through nine in this book.) A year later I found that indeed, it was useful and helpful to other healers who added the crucial elements of this type of healing. I documented the proof as a part of the thesis for my masters degree, which I completed at Goddard College in 1987.

Possibilities For Healing Our Culture

Opportunities to use this work abound in many fields of endeavor. Creative people in churches and temples, education, psychology will find countless ways to address and truly heal the child within. Loving and giving people in many walks of life will find new ways to express their love.

Childhood is no longer a part of life that cannot be altered. Our personalities do not need to forever accept and adjust to conditions as they were imposed upon us. We have a birthright of emotional health, and a natural inclination to move towards greater health. The psychologist Abraham Maslow describes the human drive to progress from meeting basic needs such as food and sex to the highest needs of self-actualization, when we fulfill our greatest human potential. For the <u>first</u> time in history, we have the opportunity to right the wrongs from our childhoods. We all now have the possibility of having a good childhood under our belts, and then reaching our potential. Our ages do not matter. Time and space mean nothing to the child within.

I believe that the world <u>will</u> be a better place. M.Scott Peck, M.D., Ph.D, the author of <u>The Road Less Traveled</u>, teaches an awareness of love, psychological development, and spirituality. He notes that those who suffer from great voids in infancy, very dependent people, are frequently unaware or unconcerned with spiritual growth. That was true for me. I needed the experience of human love in the core of my being before I discovered God.   M. Scott Peck further states that "the only true end of love is spiritual growth or human evolution."   I believe that we will have human evolution as more and more peoples' voids are filled.

Also, who knows what genius will be offered to the world as the most damaged are brought to health, from children to elders? Each person has a unique and special gift to contribute to the world. These gifts will be uncovered as more people heal. What if all were healed? How many latent Helen Kellers, Einsteins, Mahatma Gandis, and Martin Luther Kings would be set free from the confines of their missing building blocks, and make their contributions to the world? With commitment and giving from many loving people, we can halt, and then eradicate, the famine of the heart that has hurt so many.

After I began to heal with Sam, I began testing him. Once I got beyond my tremendous fears of rejection, the fun began for me. It was not so much fun for him. After some time my demands got out of line. I gleefully filled his whole answering machine with messages. No one else could leave a message for him because I had filled the whole thirty minute tape. He responded with new limits; he told me to stop calling him until he said I could call again.

So then I had fun writing to him. I wrote postcards and letters to him. I teased him unmercifully about his shortcomings, many of which I saw. I also sent him a check for a million dollars, because Sam truly gave me a life worth living. Luckily he didn't cash it, as I only had two dollars in my account!

People and animals that do not feel loved wish to die or do die. Sam saved me with his warm arms and loving ways.

I used a postscript in the letters I sent him that I will share. It fits my dream of seeing the famine of the heart ebb. It matches my dream of seeing people's eyes shine as they heal and grow. It fits my dream of seeing leaders of the churches perceiving all religions as sisters, appreciating the core beliefs they share, while acknowledging the beauty of the differences. It matches my dream of political leaders working with integrity for the benefit of all. It fits my dream of responsible people caring for and healing the planet. It corresponds with my dream of a world that works for everyone, with no one left out. Here is the postscript that I sent in those letters to my healing partner. Don't you think that it fits these dreams?

P.S. I believe in Magic (love)

Bibliography and Resources:
The Road Less Traveled, by M. Scott Peck_A beautiful book about people who are committed to heal.

Chapter 3

Building A Human Being
Filling the Building Blocks in Childhood
The Shortcomings in our Culture

Each of us has had some building blocks filled and some left empty, on the vast continuum that begins when we are in the womb and stretches until we leave this life. There are many educational and psychological theories that explain our state of being, from many a viewpoint.

Little attention has gone into the study of healthy and happy people. If successful, healthy mothers and fathers had been studied and heard, perhaps the simple truths would have been discovered years ago.   We learn truth from simplicity. Don't we humans complicate simple things?

One way to describe the continuum where we all reside is to use a metaphor of a skyscraper to represent our completed or empty building blocks of emotional, spiritual and intellectual development. To build a skyscraper, first the foundation is prepared. The foundation represents the intellectual, emotional, and spiritual thoughts and atmosphere that lead to our conception, and then our fetal life. The first few stories of the skyscraper portray our first year of life. We can think of some rooms on these bottom floors as being lovingly furnished and attended, while others remain vacant. Some rooms may show battlescars of traumas that occurred in this first year of life. Some rooms may have only the bare skeleton of the steel framework to hold the building and the upper floors intact.

The conditions of the conception, fetal life, and first year of life vary enormously from one person to another. This results in the continuum of well-being that is the foundation for either a stable and happy life, or the misery that we call chronic mental illness. These are the most important times in the life of a child for creating this firm foundation and strong basic structure.

The ideal caretakers are at least one loving male and one loving female. The ideal result after conception, birth, and the first year of life are all of the rooms lovingly filled in and attended by loving male(s) and female(s). This rarely happens in our culture. Babies frequently have to adapt to over-busy, over-stressed parents. They are born and handled to adapt to the doctors' and hospitals' needs. They may be drugged and separated from their mother at birth, interrupting a nine-month continuous contact. Then when they are taken home, the conditions vary from constant warm, loving care to almost total abdication of care. According to T. Berry Brazelton, M.D., pediatrician and the author of numerous books on infant and child well-being, in his new book <u>Touchpoints</u>, says on page 235 that "our present culture does not adequately nurture and protect new parents." When parents lack adequate support, they can give less to their children. The children feel the strain.

The following additions to the skyscraper are very important also, with the completion and filling in of the lower floors paving the way for better completion and filling in of the upper floors. We can think of five additional levels of our skyscraper representing the five stages of development beyond infancy. Our completed building, representing us as the adult, is unique in our particular combination of filled rooms, vacant rooms, and rooms possibly battlescarred or in skeletal form.

Each of us is raised in an emotional atmosphere, deep in relationship to our main caretakers. We are not mechanical beings that just need a little food every so often, as a car needs gas and oil.

I formulated the following ideas regarding bonding energy during my healing process. The major emotional energy that enables us to fill in our building blocks with our main caretakers, usually our mother and father, a term I call "bonding energy." It is an energy with which we are born, and has us form tight bonds at the first opportunity. When the opportunities to bond closely to a warm male and warm female are not there, this bonding energy remains in wait, available to use whether we are one year old or fifty years old. My theory is that the unused bonding energy is what enables us to recreate experiences from infancy to adolescence, fill in the missing building blocks at a later time, and heal. The unused bonding energy is also what enables us to survive when those building blocks are not satisfied. It helps us block our awareness of those needs and go on the best we can with our life. Dr. T. Berry Brazelton speaks of just how rapidly an infant can begin healing. On page 247 of Touchpoints he describes an eight month old infant hospitalized for environmental deprivation. With no nurture in the home, even when food is given, these little babies do not gain weight. With a nurturing hospital staff giving it attention, this infant began to gain weight, learn trust in people, and learn cognitive lessons in ten days!

Our entire growth and development thrives with our ability to bond with our caretakers. The bonding energy changes form in the six stages of childhood. It is most intense in infancy, and, if enough needs are met, changes more and more to independence and interdependency in each succeeding stage of childhood. When people are not available for bonding, the infant might bond with objects. The objects might be anything at hand that offers comfort, such as a bottle, stuffed animal or blanket. When little or no bonding with caretakers is available, this causes a complete lack of building blocks in the first year of life. My parents were so unavailable physically, when I was left alone for long hours, that I bonded to a stuffed animal. That gave me some comfort in the long hours I was left alone.

There is nothing wrong with a normal baby attaching to these comfort-giving items in addition to his bonding with caregivers. They can be important means of the baby learning to nurture itself. However, in my case the human bonding was mostly left out of the picture.

In the book by Harlow called <u>Learning to Love</u>, baby monkeys were separated from their mothers. They were offered a wire or cloth substitute mother. They clung to the cloth substitute. Some comfort is better than none.

One of the most intensive studies of bonding was undertaken by John Bowlby. In his book <u>Attachment and Loss</u>, Bowlby describes the bonding that instinctively happens in many animals and humans. He points out that we take it for granted that we see cows with their calves, ducks and ducklings, and that we assume that they will stay together. As humans mature more slowly, we need an extended time with our caregivers.

Abraham Maslow, the American psychologist well known for his self-actualizing theory, theorized that each person has a hierarchy of needs that must be satisfied. These range from basic physiological requirements to love, esteem, and finally, self-actualization. As each need is satisfied, he theorized, the next higher level becomes conscious. For example, people who lack food or shelter or do not feel safe are unable to express the higher growth of self-actualization.

Maslow based his theory on healthy people who used all their potential rather than studying disturbed people. This ties in well with my theory that basic building blocks must be filled for people to function, and that filling those building blocks in many people in our population will help empty our jails and mental hospitals, and enable many more of us to contribute to our culture.

If all of our needs were met, and our metaphorical skyscrapers were full of lovely, completed rooms (completed emotional building blocks), I believe that we would grow up to be very loving people, equally balanced in our abilities to feel emotions deeply and passionately, and to think clearly in all situations. We would be able to contribute in a positive way to others. However, most of us fall short of this ideal.

Each of us has a unique combination of thinking and feeling. Some people, early in their formation, learned to think clearly. Other people perceived thinking to be a danger to their survival, and decided (when they were only two feet tall, and knew almost nothing about the world) that they would not think, to one degree or another. Other people decided (when they were only two or three feet tall) that they would suppress emotions.

We all are somewhere on the pendulum of thinking versus feeling when we have gaps in our development. Have you ever met people who function superbly in the work environment, and are at a complete loss in their home and social life? Or vice versa? Someone who is a master of social skills, has tremendously loving personal relationships, but is unable to function well in the business aspects of life? Blame it on those missing building blocks again! As we fill in the gaps, we can think more and more clearly in more and more situations, and feel deeply in more areas without being overwhelmed by our emotions.

Our perception of reality is tremendously affected by gaps or filled building blocks in the six stages of development. People who have great gaps in their foundation and first year of life will perceive the world as a dangerous place. They will not trust others, as they never had the basic building blocks of trust in that first year of life. They will have a great sense that something is wrong with themselves, that they are fundamentally wrong, and should not exist. This is the natural result of not having these all-important basic needs met, and why suicide is always an issue in their lives.

People who have more of the building blocks filled in infancy, but lack those immediately following will perceive themselves as unworthy, and see others as more worthy than themselves. Or they might flip this the other way, and see themselves as the only worthy one, the only right one, and everyone else as untrustworthy or wrong.

As more and more of the building blocks are filled in, people will feel good about themselves, and will have a growing circle of others who they trust and love and accept.

I will share a beautiful example of someone who had many of these building blocks filled in all of the six stages of development. There was a woman who called herself Peace Pilgrim. She saw something good in even the worst person. Video tapes of her speaking engagements are available, as well as a book and pamphlet. In particular, a video entitled "Peace Pilgrim speaking to college classes at Cal State Univ. of L.A." is pertinent. In it she mentions many of the well-known leaders in psychology, such as Freud, Maslow and Erick Fromm. She points out that their theories and methods address the different stages of development.

Severe gaps or traumas in the building blocks of the foundation and first year cause chronic mental illness. These problems are described with multi-syllable labels. Some of those labels are psychosis, schizophrenia, multiple personality disorder, borderline psychosis, manic depressive disorders, and "chemical imbalances."

Another way to describe these problems is that they are simply variations of building blocks of the 'foundation and first stories' of our metaphorical building which are unfulfilled. The bonding energy that is not used to bond closely to caretakers is then used in various creative ways to survive with those particular missing building blocks.

Hallucinations and delusions can also be viewed differently. They can be seen as the safe expression of fear and other emotions, created with the unused bonding energy in order to survive. These emotions or thoughts are not safe for the person to experience in his body or mind, due to the home situation and gaps in his foundation building blocks. So they are experienced as "outside" of the body or mind.

Suicide is always a part of the makeup of someone who is mentally ill. This is because they were unable, for a wide variety of reasons, to receive love as an infant. They are therefore unable to receive love from others in grown-up ways. In addition, they are usually not receiving the infant love experiences many of them are missing, and often lead loveless, miserable lives.

What then, is needed for healing minor to major voids in our building blocks? First needed is the awareness that we have voids, and that it is possible to fill them. The second step is desire to fill our voids. The third step, and perhaps the most important, is the belief that you will succeed. Finally, with this belief of success, you can create a vision of the pleasure that you will feel and the life that you will lead when these voids are filled. My belief and the vision of a life filled with love was what sustained me through the years of failure and harsh treatment. I still hold that vision in front of me to aspire to more and more love in my life, and more and more satisfying work, growth, and healing.

I believe that the world works on love. I think that it is only our errors or lack of knowledge and understanding, and choices that we make that prevents humans from living lives of love. In the beautiful book, <u>Beginning to See</u>, the author Sujata says that it is hard to be constantly loving. Then he points out that it is harder not to. What do you think?

Bibliography and Resources:

a video entitled "Peace Pilgrim speaking to college classes at Cal State Univ. of L.A," c. 1982, Friends of Peace Pilgrim, 43480 Cedar Avenue, Hemet, CA 92544. Peace Pilgrim speaks of how different well known psychologists addressed different stages of development.

<u>Attachment and Loss</u>, Vol. 1, John Bowlby, c. 1969, Basic Books, Inc., NY.
A well-referenced book, honored among scholars in the fields of human sciences, regarding attachment behavior in human children.

<u>Beginning to See</u>, Sujata, c. 1987 by Stillpoint Institute, Celestial Arts, P.O. Box 7327, Berkely, CA 94707.
A book teaching love of self and others, and beginning meditation.

<u>Learning to Love</u>, Harry F. Harlow, c. 1971, Albion Publishing Co., San Francisco, CA. This book

describes how primates relate with affection or the lack of it.

Peace Pilgrim, c. 1982, Friends of Peace Pilgrim, 43480 Cedar Avenue, Hemet, CA 92544. An inspiring book about a woman whose entire life became a prayer for peace, beginning in the 1950's. She single-handedly may have inspired the widespread peace movements that we have today.

T. Berry Brazelton, M.D., <u>Touchpoints</u>, c. 1992, Addison-Wesley Publishing Co., Reading, Massachusetts.
A book written by a loving pediatrition regarding important moments in the lives of new babies and parents, and pediatrician interaction.

Chapter 4

A Vision Of Love In Action

"Stranger in a strange land
Filipino maid Scrubbin'
someone else's floor On her
knees she slaves"

"Who will hold her when she cries
Who will understand
Who will see the child inside
Her tired aching hands"

"Who loves the least of these
Servant all alone
from musical recording
Who loves the least of these
"Stranger in a Strange Land
Stranger far from home"   by Andy Landis

The Healing Partner's Qualities And Skills

Certain qualities are very desirable in the healing partners. These qualities are most important when dealing with people who are missing the building blocks from birth to one year. They are going to be the most sensitive and the least trusting of those who seek help. Those who need the building blocks in the rest of the childhood stages will be correspondingly less critical of the caregivers' shortcomings, stage by stage.

The most important qualities in the caregiver to fill the voids in the early stage are warmth, understanding, gentleness and the ability to listen and observe very well. A new relationship must form, and the healing and the effectiveness of the techniques all take place within the boundaries of this new bonding, this new relationship. This may mean a dedicated hour once a week, or more time for those who have more to give.

If there is no new bonding in the relationship between the healing and receiving partners, the statements that can create a new mental structure (defined in chapter six) will be powerless. They are not magic words. The magic comes from the healing power of love in the new relationship.

People can only give what they have to give. Sam was unable to give me some of the building blocks I needed. But from our relationship, I grew from never having trusted anyone to trusting him. I gained the ability to distinguish trusting, loving and trustworthy people from others who were not trustworthy or loving. Also, I regained the ability to feel hunger and almost all of my emotions, except hurt. I began to feel good most of the time, and acquired a skeletal structure of health with which to relate to the world. I learned many problem solving tools. With this progress I was able to go to college, at long last. I acquired the ability and the opportunity through Sam to give what I had gained to others. Sam wasn't perfect, but I gained a life worth living, and an ability to give to others.

My next major healer, a woman, also lacked some of the building blocks I needed. She was also unable to fill all of my voids. But I gained a wonderful sense of being loved and being special, and much healing in regards to women. I had a great increase in my long-term loving relationships with women friends.

All of us are human and imperfect. I encourage people to do the best they can, and give what they can give. Intent and a commitment from the heart go a long way. People can accept your shortcomings if you are honest and open.

A good model for the basic atmosphere for this healing process can be seen on the listening expert, Carl Rogers. He is no longer living, but tapes showing him giving sessions are available. Just add holding, feeding, emotional release, and statements that can create new mental structure to Carl Roger's style of lovingly listening, and that is the healing environment needed.

I have purposely omitted the names of those who have been my healing partners. It would be easy for healers reading this to forget that the original answers for this healing came from the people needing healing. When Jacqui Lee Schiff asked her schizophrenic client what he needed, he curled up on her lap and cried like a hungry baby. He provided the clue. She was smart and daring enough to listen and recognize his need, and got a baby bottle and fed him! Sam had great skills in listening. He observed and heard how important I believed being held and fed were for me. My point is, after learning the basics, your <u>clients</u> will be your best teachers, if you are very open, and <u>look</u> at them and <u>listen</u> to them!

The most important step you can take before offering this type of healing to others is to experience it yourself. If you want to hold other people, find someone to hold you first. If you want to feed others, find out what it feels like to be an adult "getting little" and getting fed. Ask for the statements that can create new mental structure (see chapter six) to be said to you. Let your vulnerable feelings out, with a safe healing partner. Then ask to be held. Let warmth from another person replace the feelings you just let go.

The ultimate keys to opening each person to health are within that unique person. Each person had a different childhood, and closed himself a little differently. Although you can learn techniques from other healers, the real expert on his own healing is your client. Help him learn to listen to what is within him, and draw it out.

Expert listening is where the relationship begins. Skilled listening is where emotional learning and healing begin. The details of the advanced listening skills required for healing partners are in chapter eight. This information would also be helpful to anyone wishing to relate more closely to a spouse or child, or to lower stress on the job by learning new responses to the boss and fellow employees.

The Power of the Healing Partner's Words

Dr. Thomas Gordon, in his book <u>Parent Effectiveness Training</u>, taught the use of "I" statements. This is a crucial skill for this type of healing. Incorrect "you" statements can undermine the healing process. They can cause incorrect new mental structure to be formed. If the caregiver trains herself to use <u>only</u> "I" statements, with a very few and specific exceptions described in chapter six (creating new mental structure), it will help her avoid many a pitfall in this healing method.

Here are some examples of "I" statements. The judgmental aspect of saying "you did this" is avoided.

> I feel uncomfortable when I am lectured.
> I feel sad when I hear that.
> I am unwilling to be around criticism.
> I am feeling pushed by the demands I am hearing.

Words have power! This is an incredible discovery, and one of the most important keys to this healing. Many healers are unaware of the incredible power exchange that occurs when one person is dependent on another. When doctors tell terminally ill patients that they are going to die, their words, if believed, become the death sentence.

The words of a caregiver in this healing process can be tremendously magnified in power for some people. The power of the healing partner's words can vary from one receiving person to the next. For some clients, your "you" statements may have tremendous power. For others, they won't at that time, and may or may not have power at another time. This is a very important key to the caregiver's effectiveness. This phenomenon of words sometimes having power, and which words, is absent in all of the literature on healing that I have found, with the partial exception of Jacqui Schiff's work.

Some examples of "you" statements that use the imperative, or the 'you understood' form:

Have a nice day.
Stop that.
Do this job for me.

Other "you" statements contain "you" itself as the subject. Here are some examples:

You should not go to that part of town by yourself.
You should think for yourself.
You shouldn't clean house for her.

For this type of healing, I discovered that certain specific "you" statements are helpful. I found out that others can cause harm and delays in healing. They are listed in Chapter Six.

In her book, <u>All My Children</u>, Jacqui Schiff tells how she became aware that clients became "bound" to her words, and would take her words literally. She discovered the first part of the power of words, that some people are tremendously affected. She learned not to tell jokes or tease, unless it was specifically identified as such.

The further discovery that I made was that these original pioneers overused the "you" statements, and did not discover the harm or impediment to progress that was caused. One of the most important aspects of training to be a great caregiver is to avoid the use of <u>all</u> "you" statements except those that are absolutely needed for functioning. They will be listed below.

For all people who strive to relate in the most beneficial, rewarding, and positive ways, it is best to avoid "you" statements. "You" statements are needed with children, and some are needed in this healing process. But in other adult relationships they can cause discomfort or resistance to your input. If you wish to be heard, my suggestion is to frame your input as a request or a suggestion. Before making a suggestion, you might first asking if the person would like your input. In a nutshell, here are the steps to take:

Ask if a suggestion would be welcome.
Example: Are you receptive to a suggestion about your project?
Or, make a request.
Example: I'm feeling scared driving so close to the car in front of us. Will you please move to the other lan or leave more distance between our car and the one in front?

Avoiding "you" statements is not as easy as it sounds. "Take care of yourself," and "Have a good week," are mistaken "you" statements for this type of healing process.

This lack of awareness of the power that healers have with their words reminds me of the situation in medicine a hundred years ago. Doctors and midwives didn't know that dirty hands spread disease. When they were first told that cleaning hands was important, many scoffed in disbelief. They couldn't see the germs, and didn't believe that their unwashed hands had the power to do harm.

This is a parallel situation. Many healers do not know or believe that their words have power. They may not have experienced this power themselves. Their lack of awareness does not mean that their words lack power, either to help or to harm.

With awareness, openness and true listening, and being open for and asking for feedback from the client, the healer can steer the course with more precision. This is also the only way the profoundly damaged can be healed in any numbers. They are too fragile to withstand many errors, or the burden of any extra "you" statements.

Caregivers who want to offer the full power of these healing experiences will need to discover the power of their words. It is difficult to believe something that you have not experienced. We often accept the value of an experience when it has meaning for us personally.

A caregiver who is able to follow the instructions about the "you" statements and the "I" statements diligently will be able to see the results in his receiving partners. I am not asking healers to believe this, but I am asking you to test this for yourself. When the basics of this healing process have been in place, with careful listening, diligence in avoiding "you" statements, and a gentle, understanding, safe atmosphere is in place for a period of time, you can test.

After offering the statements that can create a new mental structure, you can ask your clients if they remember any of your words, and ask which ones. Then you will have proof. Some of the receiving partners will list the new "you" statements word for word as they were given.

During my internship, I once asked a client what his previous psychologist, whom he had seen for many years, had told him he "should" do. He spoke for about thirty minutes, reciting everything the man had told him he "should" do. He was bound to those words, and tried to carry them out. He was greatly relieved when I told him to forget all of those words and his parents' words, and to only remember the less burdensome ones I would tell him.

When I interviewed a woman who received

this type of healing from someone I had taught, I was stunned at the results. I had given the facilitators a one-page typed list of the healing "should" statements, the statements that can create new mental structure. This particular healer read one statement a week to her client, until she got to the bottom of the list.

I asked the client, who had progressed wonderfully in a year of treatment, what words of importance her healer said to her. Luckily I had a tape recorder playing! She repeated the words from the page I had given her healing partner verbatim, word for word!

These few "you should" statements can create a new internal mental structure for the person being healed. They are leaving behind a more limiting mental structure, which needs something to replace it.

I was tremendously sensitive to the "you should" (imperative) statements, which is how this discovery came about. In addition, Sam almost never used "you" (or imperative) statements. I asked him to tell me "should" statements as it occurred to me that I needed to hear them, one at a time.

When I asked for a "you" statement from Sam, and it was a mistake, I would have immediate strong reactions. One such simple mistaken "you" statement was "Take care of yourself." My body became very uncomfortable, and I lost the new ability I had just gained to feel my emotions.

I only had to call Sam, and ask him to tell me to forget the specific words he told me. That "you forget" statement worked! Within a few minutes I felt better! I was the original guinea pig, and suffered from our mistakes in this pioneering effort. I hope to share the hard lessons I learned so that others will not have to suffer.

Other people may not overtly show the signs of stress that I did, but in the presence of too many "you" statements, they may simply never open up and grow.

An attitude of "not knowing" will keep the caregiver attentive to the receiving partner, who knows her reaction to what has transpired. Virginia Satir left a beautiful legacy of honoring the receiving partner. She realized and communicated by her attitude in taking new clients' histories, that they were the true experts on their life and their history. Caregivers would benefit by reading some of her books, such as Conjoint Family Therapy, and learning this lesson.

If a caregiver notes an adverse reaction to a healing session, it may be helpful to ask, "Did I say something to you that had special impact?" The receiving partner may be able to say specifically what was said. The caregiver can then say, " Forget the words xx yy zz that I said." If the words were the problem, the receiver will feel better within a few minutes.

I always knew that the words that I asked for were important. They seemed to be written in my brain. Later other people were to use the same words, that these words were written in their brain.

This phenomenon is not only seen with very needy people, as I was. I gave a session to a healer who had a good childhood. At one point I told her, "You don't need to take care of me." She sat up straight and looked at me, and said that it felt like her brain was being re-wired! She said, "I needed to hear that!" This may have been the only one of the "you" statements that she needed.

Some people find these words powerful immediately. Some never do. Others find them helpful only during a certain time period and not in others. I suggest giving the client all of the information about these words, so they can be alert to any discomfort at an inadvertent statement, and call you to correct it.

Some receiving partners will have only a minor empty building block in the first year of life, and your use of "you" statements may not affect them unless they are particularly sensitive. However, those who have a greater need or sensitivity may react visibly to incorrect "you" statements. They may draw their body in tightly, showing distress in their body language. Their eyes may stop shining, if they had been.

When the receiving partner who has many missing building blocks begins to trust the healing partner, a tremendous transfer of power occurs. The words and treatment given by the healing partner will assume magnified importance. The receiving partner is now as fragile and vulnerable as the hurt infant they once were. Because survival has always seemed questionable to this person, he may experience this as having his life in the hands of the healing partner. This is why he may experience mistakes as life-threatening. To him it is life-threatening, because his life of health may truly be beginning. Mistakes plunge him back into his old nightmare of a life. People with less of a need might just feel and express anger towards the healing partner for a mistake, or not even be bothered by it.

Danger of Denial in Healers

Sometimes people don't recognize the damage and fragility in people who have been terribly hurt as children and who are missing major building blocks of love and trust. This is a denial of reality, simply because it is not that person's reality.

It hurts to be missing huge building blocks of love. And it hurts to be an emotionally or physically battered child. Those hurts don't go away by themselves, even if years have gone by.

Doctors of accident victims recognize the fragility of their patients' conditions. They can see the broken bones. Healers of emotional wounds need to realize that their clients are just as damaged.

Having traveled this path myself, I can often spot emotionally damaged people by the tight muscles around their eyes, the lack of shine in their eyes, chronic shallow breathing, tight chest and stomach muscles, and rigid body movements. Other times I get clues by what the hurt person says or does.

When eyes and ears and hearts are open, the hurt can be seen. I was sometimes told by healers that I was strong because of what I survived. I cannot agree. Those hurts were healed by telling new parent figures about those hurts, and having their sympathy that I was treated badly. It was like being a small child and having my hurt finger "kissed better" by a loving mommy or daddy.

Denial of hurt never made anyone stronger or healed anything.

A healer's ability to see and comment on a healthy area, or the beautiful, childlike aspects of the receiving partner can help these areas grow. An appreciation and acceptance of the receiving person's state of being by the healing partner will help the receiving partner begin to honor himself.

The healing partner can acknowledge the intelligence of the childhood decisions that led to the present state of dysfunction in the receiving partner, since those decisions helped him survive or adapt. Then the receiving partner can begin acknowledging that they did the best that anyone could have under their circumstances.

The healer can point out the differences between this new environment and the childhood environment. These acknowledgements honor the person for being just as they are. When both partners honor how the person is right now, then it is time to add new areas of growth to appreciate. This helps build an atmosphere of mutual respect, gentleness, understanding, and caring.

When I became a co-healer with Sam, our goal was to give the receiver the best hour of his life by means of our attention and feedback. I overdid praise and compliments at first, and had to learn to give them at the level of the receiving partner's ability to take them in.

M. Scott Peck has a wonderfully sensitive ability in this area. He manages to see the highest and the best in people. Then they can begin to see it in themselves. I suggest reading his book, <u>The Road Less Traveled</u>, for examples of this.

The healing that I describe occurs within the new bonding of an ongoing relationship.

The main ingredients in this type of healing are a loving, caring,committed, bonded relationship, expert listening skills, the new mental structure provided by the new "you" statements, correction of mistaken "you" statements, emotional release of past hurts, and the opportunity to receive the baby feeding and nurturing and other childhood experiences that are missing. If any of the ingredients are missing, the healing will be correspondingly less powerful and profound.

Later in this book are journal excerpts showing my perception of this process as I began to heal, trust, and feel good for the first time in my life. I needed to learn all of life anew, as a new child within me was born.

Having my childhood as an adult was a very lovely thing to experience, and in a way I am lucky. Not everyone can remember as much of their infancy and childhood love, play and learning experiences as I can. My childhood happened when I could read, write, and remember.

Bibliography and Resources:

"Stranger in a Strange Land," by Andy Landis, from her cassette album "Stranger," c. 1993, Star Song Communications, P.O. Box 150009, Nashville, Tennessee 37215.

Carl Rogers , The Carl Rogers Institute for Peace, 1125 Torrey Pines Rd, La Jolla, CA. Telephone: (619) 459-3864

<u>All My Children</u>, by Jacqui Schiff

<u>Conjoint Family Therapy</u>, by Virginia Satir, c. 1967, Science and Behavior Books, Inc., Palo Alto, CA. The primer of family therapy. Virginia Satir discusses the changing relationships of clients and professionals from one where the professional has a superior attitude, to one of respectful equals.

<u>Parent Effectiveness Training</u>, by Dr. Thomas Gordon.

<u>The Road Less Traveled</u>, by M. Scott Peck, C. 1978, Simon & Schuster, NY.

Chapter 5

What Leaves The Voids Within?

> "I'm willing to open my eyes
>   to see your innocence.
> A child of God are you,
> a mirror of myself."
>   by Donna Marie Cary, modified
>   by the Devotional Singers in
>   Encinitas, California

The voids within all of us are left in the gaps where our childhood needs were not filled. In order to fill those voids, we need to know what goes in them. We need to know what fulfills those needs in infancy and childhood. Then, as adults, we can, if we choose, find a healing partner to help us fill those voids.

Satisfying Needs In Children

In the six stages of childhood emotional development, the child needs different responses from the parents or parent figures in order to satisfy current needs. Then the child can move on to the next stage of development. This same natural progression occurs in this healing process. When needs are satisfied in an early stage, the adult being healed usually moves on to be healed in the succeeding stage of development. Sometimes, however, an adult may jump around from one stage to another. One stage may be safer to deal with initially, and a more difficult stage may be handled later in the healing process.

Books and resources mentioned in the sections on healing the voids in adults are good books for healthy children, as well. The books were written for normal children. These books and other resources for parents will be noted at the end of the chapter.

Satisfying Needs In Children From Birth To Six Months

From birth to six months of age, a baby will either develop trust or mistrust from the pattern of responses that he receives. His first need is for the satisfaction of hunger, and bodily comfort. His next need is to form a strong bond with a warm woman and man. These will form the basis of the dependent relationships necessary for him to receive satisfaction of his emotional, developmental, and spiritual needs throughout the six stages of his childhood. When these needs are satisfied, the baby develops a foundation that will later be called trust. He will perceive the world to be a good place, that his needs are important, and that he can cry and then be nurtured in a way that feels good. Human babies and toddlers need much holding in arms. I suggest <u>always</u> honoring that request in the first six months, and as frequently as possible thereafter. Hold your baby and young child. Offer him or her as much of the paradise that only the mother and father, or parent figure can give, being held in your arms.

There is a wonderful book for parents called <u>The First Three Years of Life</u>, by Burton L. White. Healthy, loving parents were studied, and their discipline noted. The tips in that book will offer you a way to have a well-behaved child without having to use harsh, harmful discipline.

Satisfying Needs In Children From Six To 18 Months

In the second stage of development, from age six months through about 18 months of age, the baby begins to turn into a toddler, and needs to explore a rich and safe environment. Some conditional attention and limits are now appropriate. (No, you cannot chew on that electric cord, here's a toy instead. No, you cannot bite mommy, you can sit on the floor for awhile now.)

Approximately two thirds of the attention he receives should remain positive and unconditional. To be responsive to these exploratory needs, and yet provide safety, parents can baby-proof the house, with dangerous areas blocked. Parents can allow the toddler to initiate contact when he needs attention, and when he wants to leave and return to the parent in new situations. Pleasant meals with a variety of foods, patience, and parents who are responsive to their own needs are helpful in this stage.

Satisfying Needs In Children From 18 Months To Three Years

In the third stage of development, from 18 months to three years, the thinking part of the personality begins to be functional to a great degree. The child needs information and reasons; a way to express <u>all</u> feelings; limits set in a caring way; toilet training; a continuation of some positive attention; and time spent doing pleasurable activities with the parent figures.

The needs in this stage will be unsatisfied if the parent does things for the child that the child can do for himself, including some problem-solving. If expectations are too high or too low; if parenting is inadequate, inconsistent, or competitive, needs will be unmet. Also, if the child is allowed to hit peers or parents, go out of control, or control the parents, needs will be unmet.

Satisfying Needs In Children From Three To Seven Years

In the next stage of development, from approximately age 3 to 7, the child begins to test his own power. Parenting that satisfies the needs in this stage include help separating fantasy from reality; and allowing the child to do what he can for himself, including some problem-solving. A child's budding awareness of sexuality and gender need clear and correct information. He needs to know that his own body is okay, and gain age appropriate information about privacy and safety, and learn caution rather than fear. He needs to know the reasons for rules, and do a reasonable amount of arguing about the rules.

Satisfying Needs In Children From Seven To Twelve Years

The child needs to learn tools to argue and negotiate in a way that takes other people into consideration. He needs to have many experiences in doing things. This is a great time for scout clubs and team sports. Much of the child's interest will be on the rules. He needs to learn the reason for rules, and be permitted to argue about the rules. Guidelines that help the child develop, think, and take personal responsibility are needed. The child needs to learn about the negative aspects of the world. He needs to learn that not all people do good things to other people, and that there are people in the world who hurt others, animals, and the earth. Without scaring himself, he needs to learn ways to judge people and situations, and learn how to exit from negative situations, and protect himself from danger. He needs to learn to finish tasks.

Satisfying Needs In Children From Twelve To Eighteen Years

The child needs to be trusted and accepted unconditionally for himself. Misbehavior need not be accepted, but the child himself must have this acceptance. He needs to receive clear sexual information and knowledge of protection. He will begin to have sexual fantasies. He may or may not have sexual experiences. He will re-visit all of the previous developmental stages. He needs to realize that he is responsible for the outcomes of his choices. He ultimately needs to separate from his dependency on parents, and become independent. Parents need a firm foot on their values, and to be skilled in offering choices that lead to positive outcomes.

There is a sway in adolescence, from your teen wanting you to care for them in an infantile way again, to moodily demanding to be treated as an adult a few minutes later. This is _normal_! Hormones, very strong chemicals, are pumping through their body. They are learning to cope with strong new sexual feelings, along with a great surge for independence. Just try to respond to the shifts as well as you can! You may have a teenager with a job objecting to paying his own phone bill, while asking you to treat him as an adult.

It is helpful to point these things out in a way that does not make your teen feel wrong or embarrassed regarding these shifts. He is trying to sort out all these changes and growth in his own mind, and your comments, in a friendly, neutral tone, can help.

Peers become very important, and are indeed important for your teen's growth and development. When behavior becomes excessive, set choices that will lead your teen in the direction of moderation.

When you feel angry or concerned, that is a signal to you that it is time to set a limit and choices. Remind your teen that the choices he makes, and the outcomes of his choices will either make his life easier or harder. If he learns this now, it will help him in his entire adult life. He will take responsibility for his choices, rather than blaming others or luck.

You might point out that some people make choices of companions and behaviors that lead them to jail, hospital wards, drug treatment, while other people make choices that lead to job training, education, and rewarding careers. What will they choose?

Your expectations are very powerful with your child. Let him know that you are sure he will make good choices, and compliment him when he makes them. When he makes a poor choice, you can simply comment that you are sure there was a lesson he wanted to learn by his choice. Then compliment him for learning the lesson when he does.

The parent of a teen needs to be ready for deep sharing of concerns at odd moments feelings may be shared as the teen is taking the trash out, or on the way out to see friends. These feelings or concerns may be shared quite casually, as a way of testing the safety of your receptivity. You may be startled, and not respond. Then, after you have had time to think about the comment, you can casually bring it up again. "You said you felt sometimes that you are (good for nothing, upset, worried, whatever the comment from the teen was). Are you having a hard time at school, with friends, here at home? ..... listen..... "How can I help?" ..... listen.

Adolescence has been called the age of embarrassment. My junior high age son was embarrassed in the shopping mall. We were walking along an almost deserted hallway, and no one was near us. He asked me not to talk until we got to the car, because he was so embarrassed. When we got to the car, he told me that I had called him "honey" in public! He was afraid someone might hear me.

It is tougher now to be a teen than it ever was. Many teens are unsupervised much of the time, as both parents work. Aids is a fact of life now. One sexual contact with someone with the virus can transmit this disease, as easily as kissing someone with a cold can pass on the cold virus. Sexual contact that can be deadly in the future is a hard concept for teens to understand, as they often think that they are immortal.

Because you cannot go everywhere your teen goes, and they need to learn to make responsible decisions, the reality of Aids and its prevention must be discussed.

Perhaps you think you can skip this part of your job with your teen, thinking that he or she will remain a virgin until marriage. No matter how uncomfortable you may be discussing this subject with your teen, dealing with a dying child in the future would be thousands of times worse.

I have known several teens whose parents were <u>sure</u> that their teens were not sexually active. One had been sexually active for two years! These teens had used inadequate birth control prevention, foam, and had not used condoms with nonoxynol -9, which offers some protection against the Aids virus. Some of the teen music and some teen idols encourage sex, and encourage sex with both genders. Some young people, confused about their sexuality, and missing many building blocks of emotional health, are playing Russian roulette by leading promiscuous sex lives. The transmission of Aids is high in this age group.

Arguing about your rules and values is your teen's way of beginning to establish his own. True listening, and occasionally letting your teen win the argument is valuable for him. When you disagree with him, let him know that you appreciate his point of view, even though it differs from yours, but you will stick to yours in the home you have created. When he creates a home, he can create his own guidelines.

TV is not contributing much to your teen. How much of what is on TV or in videos is beneficial to him?

Your teen will own more of his knowledge if it is from a book. When people read information, they perceive it as their own acquisition. There is some thinking and mental work involved in absorbing written ideas. It can be absorbed at one's own pace. When people see information on a screen, they perceive it as someone else's ideas. They tend to think less about it. Leave good books and magazines in easy reach around the house. When the TV is off, and there's not much else to do, if you don't pressure your teen, he will likely start picking up books.

Reassure your teen of your unconditional love for him. Let him know that even though you may not love the same music or friends or activities, you love him, and will always love him. Kids need to hear your love spoken, and still need hugs. They may want to put their head on your lap when you read or watch TV. They just don't want these demonstrations in public, or in front of their peers.

Much idealism is present in teenagers, with a deep search for truth, and a wish to fulfill in some ways their ideals. Confusion and finding life meaningless can result when this search is stymied. Quests and experiences that lead your teen to personal discoveries of his own truth are very important. Perhaps the great souls that we admire, such as Mother Theresa and Mahatma Gandhi, discovered these values as teenagers, and expressed the values from their hearts in their lives.

Clues In Children From Birth To Six Months That Indicate Problems In Emotional Growth And Development

A baby who fails to gain weight and grow is in danger of dying. Extremely serious lacks lead to this condition. A baby that rejects closeness shows a need for help. Continuous feeding problems, including a refusal to eat, indicate lacks. Continuous crying shows a problem in this stage. Frequent bowel problems can indicate a stressed baby.

Clues In Children From Six To 18 Months That Indicate Problems In Emotional Growth And Development

A baby at the extremes, either very passive or quite hyperactive indicates problems. A nervous baby who cries easily shows a need for help. A baby who does not explore his environment and initiate interaction with others shows difficulties in growth. One with poor muscular coordination, who harms himself frequently without learning some caution shows a lack in development. Asthma and allergies can be a reaction to emotional difficulties. Asthma can mean "I am starving emotionally."

Clues In Children From 18 Months To Three Years That Indicate Problems In Emotional Growth And Development

A child who has frequent temper tantrums shows a lack in emotional development. One who loses control, bites and kicks frequently shows a need for help. A withdrawn, fearful, or passive toddler is giving clues that help is needed. A child who is not beginning to take other people's feelings into account and is still totally self-centered shows clues that there are problems and lacks in this stage.

Clues In Children From Three To Seven Years That Indicate Problems In Emotional Growth And Development

The child at the extremes of shyness or bullying with other children shows a lack in this stage. A child who lacks social skills in order to play well with children shows problems. Bed-wetting and nightmares can indicate a need for help. Refusal to eat the family meals, and an insistence on special food rituals can indicate problems. An extremely fearful child, or one with great fears when separating from the parent shows a need for help. An extremely passive or excessively "good" child may need help. School learning problems are a clue to a problem.

Clues In Children From Seven To Twelve Years That Indicate Problems In Emotional Growth And Development

A child who is excessively worried about his school or sport activity performance indicates problems in this stage. Extreme behavior problems, ongoing lying, cheating, stealing at home or school show a need for help. Lack of completion of chores and schoolwork show a problem. Physical problems, such as frequent stomach aches, headaches, and ulcers indicate higher than normal stress, and a need for help.

Clues In Children From Twelve To Eighteen Years That Indicate Problems In Emotional Growth And Development

When rules are too relaxed, the child searches for limits. They may act out to the point of police, hospital, or social service involvement in their search for limits.

When teens act out consistently, in spite of appropriate limits, underlying depression may be the cause. When teens are depressed, they don't always look depressed the way adults do. Instead, they act out over and over again. Community clinics offer low-cost help. Group treatment with peers is highly effective with teens.

If your teenager is making suicidal threats, such as "someone should just kill me," or suicidal gestures such as extreme limitation of food intake, take these signs as a red flag that immediate professional help is needed. Let his school know of your concerns. Extra support may be available there. Adolescence is a time of impulsive behavior, and a suicidal, impulsive teen needs help fast. When they decide to take action, it is often fast and without warning. Ignoring these red flags could cost your teen his life.

A delay in sexual and physical development can indicate possible problems, if in conjunction with other difficulties. A promiscuous teen may be attempting to get nurture by being sexual, and is indicating problems in this stage. A teen who is impulsive, has few inner controls regarding expression of feelings and behavior indicates lacks in development. Extreme rebelliousness or extremely passive behavior shows unmet needs. Hygiene shows a problem at the two extremes, overconcern with cleanliness, or a total lack of concern. Teens that run away rather than dealing with their problems show emotional and developmental lacks. Dependency on drugs, and on peers to the exclusion of the family indicate problems in this stage. Over-exercising and under-eating, over-eating, or excluding several food groups shows serious problems.

How Voids Are Created From Birth To Six Months

Jacqui Schiff, the pioneer of the original method of healing from which this method grew, described parental behaviors that result in needs in the first six months of life in response to hunger being unsatisfied. Here are the mechanics of the creation of profound voids that lead to eating disorders. They are:

1. Over-responsiveness
The baby only puts out minimal energy, and does not develop frustration tolerance.
2. Overfeeding
The baby associates discomfort with gratification.
3. Non-association of hunger to gratification of eating
This can occur with neglected or starving babies, handicapped babies, or premature babies, especially if tube-fed.
4. Reluctant nursing
A tense mother can inhibit the flow of milk. The baby can feel unsatisfied and frustrated.
5. Agitated feeding
The baby will feel the feeding person's agitation, and be uncomfortable.

6.   Absence of touching and nurture during feeding A baby that is left with a propped bottle, and lacks holding, touching and talking will be grossly unsatisfied.

A baby is born with what I call "bonding energy," enough to bond strongly to a warm man and woman. When he is unable to use that energy or any portion of that energy to bond, he uses that energy still available and unused to either adapt, or in more difficult situations, to survive. The development of attachment to both a female and male is a prerequisite for later successful relationships with either gender. I first formulated these ideas as I began to heal in 1980. The following is an excerpt from the journal I kept, that I called "Coming Alive."

Every baby needs two warm, caring people, one of each sex, who will feed him when he's hungry, comfort the baby when he's uncomfortable, personally take care of him a sufficient amount of the time, and form a bond with him until these baby needs are met, at approximately one year of age. If any of the above needs are unmet to the degree that it causes the baby unbearable, intolerable pain, the baby will become psychotic. Some other causes of psychosis are physical pain from accident or illness, lack of any person to bond with during the adoption process, starvation (being fed by the clock rather than by the baby's need) neglect, rejection for being the wrong sex baby for those parents, or not being wanted by those parents at that time.

In some cases, the baby is unable to form a bond with one parent, and bonds to an object instead, according to my new theory. I also theorize that some deaf-mute people with no physical impairments may be catatonic schizophrenics who heard unbearable, intolerable noise when they were newborns, and turned off hearing instead of movement, which is what most catatonic schizophrenic people block.

More new theory is that a baby is born with just enough energy to bond to a man and a woman. When that doesn't happen, I think that the baby uses that available, unused energy in a different way in order to survive in his situation. Some of these babies need to turn off some degree of feelings in order to survive, and others need to turn off some degree of their mind. (This happens with all babies, I think, to some degree. The difference is in the amount of feeling and thinking that psychotic babies need to stop, and in the degree that the bonding process is incomplete.) The extra energy that wasn' used in bonding is used to go crazy, a tool that the baby needs to use to survive, and a portion of the baby's mind or feelings and senses are cut off with that energy.

There is a limit to the amount of pain that any human being can tolerate, and when that limit is reached, life is no longer desirable and the person chooses to die. When baby needs are grossly unmet, the baby is close to the human limit of pain. Also, any unbearable, intolerable trauma in babyhood brings the baby very close to that limit.

The baby will then grow older chronologically, but his real age, the age he is emotionally, will not grow until his emotional wounds are healed and his baby needs are met.

Inappropriate sexual behaviors involving a child can result in trauma to the child as well as unsatisfied emotional needs in any stage of development. Parents discomfort with sexuality can be passed on to the child, either by repression, or by considering the child as a seducer, and inappropriately involving the child in sexual comments or behavior.

How Voids Are Created From Six To Eighteen Months

Actions that will block satisfaction of these baby and toddler needs are toilet training before eighteen months, force feeding, punishment for touching and exploring, too many "no's," too many "yesses," long restriction in a crib or playpen, emphasis on neatness, cleanliness, and performance, and constant or over-frequent initiation and stimulation from the parent or other person, including siblings.

How Voids Are Created In Children From 18 Months To Three Years

When parents do things for the child that the child could do, and solve all of his problems for him, this will block satisfaction of the need to begin thinking and problem-solving. Expecting more than the child of this age can do, or having no or low expectations causes voids. Inconsistency causes voids. Permitting the child to hit parents or others causes a void.

This is a time to learn the very basics of social control. This is the appropriate time for toilet training. Lack of expectation in this area will cause the need for this self-control to be unsatisfied. Inadequate parenting will result in voids. For example, a parent who tells his child what to do, is ignored, and does nothing is going to create a void in this stage.

Parent Effectiveness Training courses are available in many areas for parents who need help in this area. In addition, the books <u>The First Three Years of Life</u>, and <u>Parent Effectiveness Training</u> can be good guides. "Parent Magazine" offers good tips on disciplining young children, as well.

How Voids Are Created In Children From Three To Seven Years

The child's needs will be unsatisfied if he is scared or teased into behaving, and if fears are reinforced rather than explained. If the parents blame the child for their feelings and/or behavior, the child's needs will not be met. If the parent withdraws nurturing from the child, the needs will be unmet. Parental distortions of reality and prejudices are passed on to the child.

How Voids Are Created In Children From Seven To Twelve Years

When parents are competitive, the child's needs are not met. Rules that are too rigid leave no room for the child to learn to think to solve problems. Instead they must blindly follow the rules. When rules are too relaxed, the child searches for limits, and will continue to misbehave until he finds that limit.   When the parent is domineering and pushy, the child's needs get left out. When parents solve problems for the child that the child could solve, the child's needs for growth are not satisfied. Tough Love is a great support group for parents, training them to have clear guidelines and choices, learn to listen effectively, and have one consistent "bottom line" per week. You do not need to have a child in trouble to attend! You can go to avoid trouble, or just to learn. You will learn to create guidelines that allow for your child's growth, and gain many helpful ideas from other parents.

How Voids Are Created In Children From Twelve To Eighteen Years

Voids can be created by seductive parents. If the child's needs for nurturing and acceptance are ignored, his needs will be unsatisfied. Either too many rules for this age child, or an absence or removal of the rules will leave needs unmet. If parents take away all pleasures as punishment, the child may give up on solving problems. This pleasureless life will leave voids and pain.

Clues In Adults That Show Voids From Birth To Six Months

The clues in adults that show lacks in this stage of development are in chapter one. When a person's needs were partially unsatisfied, he will exhibit only one or two of the clues in any stage. When the needs were grossly unsatisfied, he will have many of the clues pointing to these voids.

Clues In Adults That Show Voids From Six To Eighteen Months

An adult whose behavior is stuck in flight, fight or freeze reactions to life has unmet needs in this stage. They will have a fear of abandonment or of being overwhelmed by another person. They will constantly try to please others whom they see as parental or authoritative. They have difficulty knowing their own boundaries.

People at the extremes of activity, either hyperactive or very passive, lifeless and listless show unmet needs here. Those who are frequently bored, and lack creative abilities show needs here. Obsessive, compulsive and hysterical behavior indicates needs in this stage.

Someone with awkward movements, unaware of his body or feelings has unmet needs. Those who are accident-prone, who frequently injure themselves show needs here. One who uses a favorite maneuver to get attention, such as acting sick or stupid or constantly happy, or acting the intellectual whiz, or always in motion, with never a rest, shows a need in this stage. Physical problems such as asthma, migraines, and vision can stem from voids in this stage. Their fear masks their anger. They project their feelings onto others.

Clues In Adults That Show Voids From 18 Months To Three Years

Adults who show a lack in this stage may have a stiff neck. They may have diarrhea frequently, or constipation, or uncontrollable discharges of energy.

They are contrary: "I can't, I won't, you can't make me." They are negative, oppositional, and controlling. They resist endlessly. When asked questions, they will control by long pauses, "I don't know," answers; the person asking the questions will feel angry.

Other people's feelings are not important to people with lacks in this stage. They are very messy or very tidy. They are either over-weight or under-weight. Their anger masks their other feelings.

They may be super-responsible, then collapse to try to get cared for. They may feel that they must be in a relationship to feel safe. In the relationship, they may try to please the partner to such an extent that they give up their own needs and wishes.

Clues In Adults That Show Voids From Three To Seven Years

An adult who acts a drama of an evil person, a person going crazy, or acting scary or powerful has unmet needs in this stage. He has nightmares, and thinks he is the cause of unrelated events happening (magical thinking).

Someone with voids in this stage looks for Santa Claus, "I wish"... "I hope"... "When things get better". He scares himself, "I shouldn't"... "I"m not allowed to."

He converts his emotions from one feeling to another, he turns his anger into hurt, joy into sorrow, fear into anger (inappropriate emotional responses).

Physical problems showing needs in this stage may be circulatory problems, chest pains and palpitations, muscular binding in the chest, and a raised or lowered metabolic rate. This person has not gotten the tools that tell him how to use the signals of his emotions to help his life.

Clues In Adults That Show Voids From Seven Years To Twelve Years

A seductive person, or one who has sexual identity problems has needs in this stage. They may be latently homosexual.   They are argumentative. Either they suffer while learning, or their performance is not good enough unless they are number one.

They do not complete tasks, or do so with great difficulty. They are harried, pleasing others, perfectionistic, and rigid. They do without thinking.

They use guilt to motivate. They ignore their feelings to get things done. They live in the past or future.

Physical problems in this stage may be ulcers, headaches, chest pains or high blood pressure. They may have muscular binding in the area of the rib cage. Males with voids in this stage may have extra fatty tissue in their breasts. Females with voids here may have a body shape more typical of males, due to distribution of their body fat.

This person does not know that he does not have to do things perfectly the first time, or that he isn't expected to already know everything.

Clues In Adults That Show Voids From Twelve To Eighteen Years

One who is a frequent sexual joke teller, or talks about his latest sexual event (fantasy or reality), shows unmet needs here. He acts blatantly seductive. He is not nurturing, he wants the "real action."

He may have acne. He may have a delay in sexual development.

He is extremely one-up, vengeful, and self-centered. He lacks intimate relationships. He continues to seek others to meet his unsatisfied needs, and becomes dependent on them. He may be depressed. He may have eating disorders.

Satisfying Childhood Needs From Birth To Six Months In Adults

The information above regarding the nurture or lack of nurture for a baby from birth to six months makes it obvious that the healing partner must be a warm, calm, and nurturing person. In order to heal these missing building blocks, the healing partner must possess the building blocks within herself or himself.

In an hour or two a week, the receiving partner can be held by the healing partner, cry and be fed a warm baby bottle of milk or goat's milk or juice in response to the cry, and be held. There will be time in a session for the receiving partner to talk afterwards, and/ or express feelings regarding the session in progress, or memories from childhood. There is no set routine. Each receiving partner can create his own routine, at his own pace.

Some people may find expressing feelings far too threatening, and may simply be held and fed week after week. There is no hurry. The main lesson to be learned by the receiving partner is the healthy infant sequence of feeling a need, asking for that need, and receiving satisfaction of that need from the healing partner.

The need is so great in humans for this early feeding and holding that the receiving partner may go on to all of the other stages, and still wish to be held and fed at some point in the treatment hour. I suggest that this request <u>always</u> be honored.

A nice introduction to being held, if there is a group setting, is to have the whole group surround the receiving partner, who lies on the floor. Then carefully, the receiving partner is lifted by the group. While holding the person, and gently rocking him or her back and forth, the group can hum a lullaby.

There are various ways to "hold" an adult, to re-create the feeling of being held as a child. One way is to sit on a sofa, and have the receiving partner sit very close, facing the back of the sofa, with knees bent. Then the receiving partner leans over the healing partner's chest, and rests his or her head on the healer's chest. The main weight of the receiving partner is on his own buttocks on the sofa next to the healer. It is useful to show the hesitant new receiving partners that they are not heavy by letting them hold the healing partner, or someone else, for a moment. The healing partner needs to have a supply of tissues handy, and also to cover his chest area with a clean, soft towel. Many tears come with this healing process.

It is important to have a clear understanding that the healing partner will care for the inner child of the receiving partner during the healing sessions, and that the receiving partner has full responsibility for his or her life outside of the session time.

The receiving partner may need to wait a few minutes after the session to "grow up" enough to drive. Homework for the receiving partner can be taking a nice bubble bath to the sound of soothing music, and finishing up with baby oil or baby powder.

Gentle massage can be a very helpful weekly adjunct to healing sessions. The safest gender for the receiving partner can be the first masseuse tried, with the other gender massaging at some point in the future. It is very important that the massages are gentle and non-intrusive.

Satisfying Childhood Needs From Six To 18 Months In Adults

The main lesson for the receiving partner to learn as an adult re-creating this stage is to become aware of the "I want" impulses within, and begin to act on them. Examples of these 'wants' are described in Chapter Seven in the Innocent Wishes section.

One exercise to open this awareness of wants and wishes is for the receiving partner to sit on the floor, soften or unfocus the eyes slightly, and look around. He may want to remove his eyeglasses. He can then move toward anything that interests him. A collection of children's toys, stuffed animals, dolls, books, coloring books and crayons, rattles and pacifiers are useful for this and the succeeding stages. Some homework for the receiving partner can be to write a list of the "wants" and the "don't wants." When wants are difficult to identify, it can be easier to start with what is not wanted.

Bottle or spoon-feeding will usually be requested by receiving partners. It is <u>always</u> important to plan time for meeting these needs. Feeding should begin with the receiving partner's request, and end when they signal that they are through. Holding should always be a part of bottle feeding.

Satisfying Childhood Needs From 18 Months To Three Years In Adults

The main lesson for the receiving partner to learn as an adult re-creating this stage is to become aware of the "I want" impulses within, and begin to act on them.

A main lesson in healing is for the receiving partner to realize that both others <u>and</u> self have needs and feelings, and to learn to negotiate. A person with Borderline Personality Disorder will need to heal this stage of development. This type of person may cling to a partner in a relationship, wanting care, and then angrily push away from the partner for not being perfect.

Some receiving partners may focus so much on others' needs that they need to focus for a time on their own, and later move on to include the other person's needs in their thinking. Another may focus only on self, and need to begin including others.

An attitude that there is plenty of time, attention and things to go around, and that skills of negotiation can be learned will be helpful. The book, <u>I Feel Guilty When I Say No</u>, by Manuel J. Smith, Ph.D., is useful here, as assertiveness tools are taught in a considerate way. There are easy dialogues in the book, identified in the table of contents, for those who don't want to read the whole book.

"I" statements are an important skill for these receiving partners to learn. A good book that has dialogues that teach "I" statements and when to use them is <u>Parent Effectiveness Training</u>, by Dr. Thomas Gordon.

A useful exercise for the healing sessions is to suggest that as the receiving partner play with toys, that they say "No" frequently, and for no particular reason. You can show them a doll or stuffed animal, and tell them to pretend that this toy loves to say no, and demonstrate. Walk the toy, and say, "No, no, no."

A useful homework assignment is to suggest that the receiving partner continue life as usual, but say "no" mentally as often as possible. ("No, I don't want to get up. No, I don't want to talk to you. No, I don't want to do this.)

Satisfying Childhood Needs From Three To Seven Years In Adults

Clear and simple guidelines are needed. Limits to keep others, self, and property safe are important. (Examples: The rule is that you can't hurt yourself, others, or the property. Here is a soft foam mat for hitting or kicking, and a soft foam bat for hitting, and soft foam balls for throwing.)

Clean-up times and rules must be set. Choices must be clear and consistent. (If you throw that toy, I'll take it away. If you don't clean up the toys, you'll have to wait while I clean them up, and I can't hold you until they are all cleaned up. If you hit her, you'll have to sit by yourself until you are ready to behave.)

Many explanations of feelings, reasons and reality are needed. Encourage questions rather than assumptions. (No, you are not a wild animal because you have feelings. All little boys and girls have feelings. I'm not going away next week because I'm mad at you. I'm taking time off to take care of myself so that I can come back and have plenty to give to you.) Give honest, age appropriate (to the inner child of the receiving partner) answers. Have children's books available on feelings and bodies. A good one is <u>"Where Did I Come From?"</u>, by Peter Mayle. A good coloring book is <u>It's O.K. to Say NO!</u>, by RGA Creation.

Good homework for this and succeeding stages is a trip to the toy or craft store. Suggest that they look for age appropriate toys for their inner child.

Satisfying Childhood Needs From Seven Years To Twelve Years In Adults

This is a time for the receiving partner to learn conflict resolution. He needs to stand up for his point of view based on his reasons. He needs to learn that there are many points of view. He needs to figure out what works versus what "is right," in his point of view. If this is quite difficult for the receiving partner, he likely has earlier voids that need filling. Good homework for this stage is to do a building project designed for the age of the inner child. Puzzles and crafts and models to build are available for the various ages, interests, and levels of difficulty needed. Discuss picking tasks that are not too hard, beyond the age of the inner child.

Satisfying Childhood Needs From Twelve To Eighteen Years In Adults

This is a time for many questions to be answered. The receiving partner will go through the adolescent sway, and may have questions and show needs that relate to the earlier stages of development. Many sexual questions will arise, and need thoughtful, informed answers, or a suggestion of where to look for more information. He needs to think about making thoughtful, informed choices regarding his sexuality, rather than impulsive ones. He will need to learn that it is alright not to do what he does not want to do, and that he can make up his own mind. He may need guidance to explore career change ideas in small steps, rather than a dramatic change. He can volunteer, "shadow" someone working in the new field of interest, or take a short course. He can gain a realistic sense of the new career idea. Then he can thoughtfully design changes in his life.

A good children's book on sexuality to have handy is <u>What's Happening to Me?</u>, by Peter Mayle. The receiving partners will be very interested in the pictures and story.

A receiving partner may become sexually interested in the healing partner. This is because the healing partner is the safest person with whom to first experience these feelings. A recognition of the beauty of the receiving partner's blooming celebration for life is appropriate. You can honor that person's feelings, and let him know that you never have sex with receiving partners. Sexual contact between a healing partner and a receiving partner is never appropriate. Stopping the healing sessions may also be inappropriate, as you may then demonstrate that this is not a safe subject to discuss. It is a time to discuss how the receiving partner can think about appropriate and safe sexual contacts.

Sexual contact between the receiving partner and the healing partner will be perceived as incestuous by the receiving partner, even if he initiated it. The need for safe parenting in this stage would be violated, and the healing of this building block would be voided if sexual relations occur. It is also against the law for professional healers to engage in sexual activities with clients.

Bibliography and resources:

Poem at beginning, original lyrics by Donna Marie Cary, from her cassette album "Real Love," c. 1992, P.O.Box 358, Owensboro, KY 42302. Telephone (502)685-2588.

Poem at beginning modified by The Devotional Singers, led by Wendy and Mark Grimwood, P.O. Box 234055, Encinitas, CA 92023, telephone (619) 632-7785.

Tough Love. The National Tough Love address is P.O. Box 1069, Doylestown, PA 18901. Telephone: (215) 348-7090. Fax: (215) 348-9874.

Send a self-addressed, stamped envelope for information about groups near you, and an assessment guide for parents. This organization was started by psychology professionals, teaching parents the skills they offer in counseling.

It is run entirely by parents, for parents. It offered me more help with my son than anything else I had tried. You can learn to be a consistent parent, be in control of your household, and stand up for your rights in your home.

No one will tell you what to do, but you will get great ideas. You will get coaching on true listening from other parents, and learn to figure out what is your responsibility rather than your older child's responsibility. You will learn to have one bottom line a week, rather than being too lax or too harsh. You will also meet some very nice parents just like you, doing the best they can. It presently costs only $2 a week in my area.

Child Development, by Neil J. Salkind, c. 1994, Harcourt Brace & Company, Orlando, Florida.

"Corrective Parenting." by Brenda Schaeffer, c. 1977, Trans-Pubs, San Francisco, CA. A chart showing ages and stages of development, needs, corrections needed, and problems in childhood by stage.

The <u>First Three Years of Life</u>, by Burton L. White, c. 1975, Prentiss Hall, NJ. Learn to discipline as you meet your baby's needs. Since most of the population had grew up in dysfunctional families, most of us need to know how to teach our babies and toddlers without damaging them. Here are loving ways that work.
<u>I Feel Guilty When I Say No</u>, by Manuel J. Smith, Ph.D., c. 1975, Bantam Books, NY,NY. This book could be titled "Tools for effective, considerate, assertive communication." This book is a wonderful addition to a home library. The dialogues can be practiced with teens, and will teach skills to the whole family.

It's <u>O.K. to Say NO!</u>, an RGA Creation, published by Playmore, Inc., Publishers and Waldman Publishing Corp., NY,NY. This is an excellent coloring book teaching bodily privacy and protection, good for all young children.

"Growth and Development." Pam Levin, c. 1974, Trans-Pubs, San Francisco, CA. This is a useful chart on emotional growth and development, by stages, including needs in each stage.

<u>Parent Effectiveness Training</u>, by Thomas Gordon, c. 1970, P.H. Wyden, NY, NY. This is the original

primer of true listening. This book teaches you to define who has the problem; you, the other person, or both of you. Then it teaches what problem-solving tool to use. The proper use of "I" statements is taught.

What's Happening to Me?, by Peter Mayle, c. 1975, published by Lyle Stuart Inc., 120 Enterprise Ave., Secaucus, NJ 07094. This is a great introduction to puberty for your adolescent. Pictures and story answer all your teen's basic questions. It claims to have the answers to the world's most embarrassing questions!

Where Did I Come From?, by Peter Mayle, c. 1973, published by Lyle Stuart Inc., 120 Enterprise Ave., Secaucus, NJ 07094. Toddlers to twelve year olds will enjoy this book. This explains the birds and the bees, with pictures.

Parent Magazine

Chapter 6

The Possibility of Creating a New Mental Structure

There are only two "shoulds" in life, two acts we must all do. What comes to mind when I say this? Many people say that the two "shoulds" are death and taxes. However, paying taxes is a choice. Those who do not pay taxes may pay the consequences instead. The only two "musts" are that we must first live until our physical body dies, and second, our physical body must someday die. Everything else is a choice.

Adults have many internal rules that help us live our life easily and somewhat automatically. For example, we do not have to decide every day if we should brush our teeth, because at some point most of us have decided to make brushing our teeth on a regular basis a "should" in our lives. This saves us time and effort, so we don't have to rethink everything in our lives every day. All of our internal rules, or "shoulds" and "shouldn'ts," "do's and don'ts" came from a decision we once made about each rule.

Some of the decisions we made regarding our personal list of rules were made thoughtfully, as adults aware of the world around us. Others were made when we were small children, toddlers. We decided on some of our "shoulds" when we didn't know anything about the world. Our only world was that of our parent figures, siblings, and those people who touched our lives directly.

Many people entering personal growth courses and therapy begin to examine their internal list of "shoulds." A friend of mine went to counseling. His counselor told him to make a list of his "shoulds" as he went about his days, and then bring the list to examine it together. The counselor took a look at the long list and told my friend, "You are 'shoulding' on yourself!" My friend took a careful look at his list and discarded most of the "shoulds." He felt as if a burden had lifted. All we really need as adults is enough "shoulds" to take care of our own well-being and to be thoughtful and caring of other people in our lives.

When other people speak to us from the position of their own "shoulds," it is often difficult for us to listen to them objectively. We often react defensively. We tend not to want to have someone else's "shoulds" imposed on us. Following is a way to step around this often unpleasant emotional impact, and turn the exchange into a pleasant and empowering one, rather than being at the mercy of others' judgements and criticisms. This skill is learning to look for and acknowledge the positive commitment, unspoken, behind the negative words.

Words of judgment and criticism are difficult for most people to handle. The skill of looking for the positive background commitment is especially valuable if the person criticizing you is in a relationship with you, your parents, spouse, children, employer, etc.

When you hear words of criticism, take some quiet time by yourself. Look <u>behind</u> the critical, judgmental words for the positive commitment. The next time you see the person, acknowledge their positive commitment to you. For example, to the mother of a single adult, who criticizes her grown son for staying out late on work nights, the son could see her commitment to his well-being, his need for enough sleep, and her commitment to his success in life, that he is rested enough to do a good job at work. He could then say to her, "I want to acknowledge your love for me, and your commitment to my health and to my success on my job. Thanks, Mother." Or to the perfectionistic, pushy boss, "Thanks for your commitment to excellence. And thanks for wanting me to do my best. I want you to know that I'm also committed to doing an excellent job for you, and to doing my best."

When you look for the positive commitment, and speak to that, you will remove yourself from the parent/child trap that we can so easily get into with authority figures. Then we uncomfortably either adapt or rebel. You will also avoid falling into the trap of returning judgment and criticism to the one who criticized you, which becomes a vicious circle. In addition, you avoid becoming entangled in thoughts that there is only one right way to speak, your way, your therapist's way, the "right" way.

Gentle Reparenting   The ORIGINAL Guide   J. Alvin

130

When I first began to heal, and regressed to childhood, I had no internal structure. The old "shoulds" from my parents were not available to me. I was unable to function in any way except as a small child. I discovered that I could ask my healing partner to tell me "should" statements. Then I could function within the parameters of that statement.

The imperative statements created a new mental structure within my mind. I could now function again. I could drive and shop and do the necessary chores of adulthood. But once necessary chores were done, I was in the state of a child. I was finally living a childhood, playing and intensely feeling my emotions, and learning. These new "you should" statements helped me function safely in that childlike state.

The imperative statements that offered me a temporary new mental structure as I healed also were to prove beneficial to other people. Sometimes people would need to hear all of the statements, as I did. Sometimes a person would only need one particular statement to help fill a missing building block from their childhood.

Here's an example of someone who only needed to hear one statement. One healer had only one experiential session with me, as an adjunct to the short class for healers I taught. He was a primal therapist, adept at working with his emotions, and releasing old feelings from his childhood. As he lay down to work with his feelings, he offered many reassuring statements to me. In response to all of the unnecessary caretaking, I told him one of the statements that was helpful to me, "You don't have to take care of me." This man sat up, and said, "I needed to hear that. I feel like something is getting re-wired in my brain!" This was a person who had experienced a fairly loving, normal childhood, rather than someone as damaged as I had been. Yet the words he needed had great power and meaning to him, and he had the same experience I had, of feeling like his brain was being re-wired.

I also had frightening experiences of mistaken statements. Fortunately my healing partner avoided the use of imperative statements much of the time.

I received most of the statements that helped me by my request, one per session. That gave me time to see how I was helped or badly affected by this statement.

However, a seemingly harmless statement from my healing partner at the end of a healing session, "Take good care of yourself" had me soon losing my emotions, my "new child." I was always aware of the latest statement from my healing partner. I experienced the words as if they were written in my brain. Later other people were to describe that exact same experience. So I called my healing partner on the phone, and asked him to tell me to forget the words "Take good care of yourself." Within about 20 minutes I returned to my childhood state, feeling my emotions again.

Another mistaken statement from my healing partner caused me enter a catatonic state. I sometimes suffered as a result of my sensitivity to these messages. But I felt that I suffered so that other people being healed after me would not have to suffer. I found the minimal number of statements supportive of emotional growth and health by trial and error. Hopefully, those following me would have only to hear the ones that are helpful.

Healers must remember that all "you" statements can cause incorrect mental structure to be formed in receptive clients. That is why it is so important for healers to use "I" statements, other than the "you statements" listed here.

Why are words so powerful for some people at times? In this healing process, it is because of a magnificent power exchange between the receiving partner and the healing partner. As the receiving partner begins to trust the healing partner, he realizes internally, probably not consciously, that he can receive the parental building blocks that he needs. He feels a sense of safety within the atmosphere created by the healing partner. This is one way a receiving partner who feels very powerless can give his power to someone he hopes can meet his needs. Babies are powerless, and the adults who care for them are very powerful. The receiving partner gives his power to the healing partner, which he will take back step by step as his early building blocks are filled, and he eventually grows up anew. The imperative words of the healing partner and the experiences in the healing sessions are magnified in importance. This provides an opportunity for the receiving partner to experience a babyhood or childhood in an hour or two a week.

Words in general can have power for children and some adults, especially if they are imperative sentences, the "shoulds" and "shouldn'ts," the "do's and don'ts," . Small children and some adults take words literally. This is an important reason to use words with care. Avoid using words in anger, for example, that say "I will kill you," or some other words implying harm. Be careful as you make jokes with small children and adults who take words literally. "Go and play in the traffic" may seem funny to you, but it can be taken as a serious message of "You are not wanted here" to a small child. It is a good idea, in general, to avoid using "should" statements to other adults. Your ideas will be better received if they are presented as suggestions rather than "shoulds."

These statements that can create new mental structure are one of the keys to this healing. People can heal when the healing partner does not know of this power. But the healing will be slower and less powerful. The receiving partner is denied the power of the minimal number of "new parent" statements that are needed, and quite possibly burdened by unnecessary imperative statements from the healing partner.

There is a danger in the power of the healing partner's words. In every arena in life, power can be used for the benefit or detriment of those affected by the power. It is the same in this case. The healer's words can be a tremendous power for healing. When this power is unknown to the healing partner, disaster can result.

For example, I once knew of a healing partner who was unsuccessful in healing suicidal clients. Finally tiring of the talk of suicide, instead of referring the clients to other help, this person told the clients to just kill themselves. They did.

There is a danger of a counselor being insensitive to the fragility within some of their receiving partners. When tremendous voids are present in the first year of the person's life, suicidal thoughts will always be an issue to be handled. "Shoulds" that create an over-heavy "new parent" may feel life-threatening to these vulnerable and perhaps very damaged people.

So this is a warning for these vulnerable people to select very sensitive people as healing partners. If you are the receiving partner in a situation that does not "feel right" to you, feel free to speak up. If the situation is not resolved, do not blame yourself. Even though leaving treatment with your healing partner may be very difficult, it may be the right thing to do. You can find a healing partner that is a better match for you.

This ability to become "bound" by the imperative statements is mentioned in Jacqui Lee

135

Schiff's first book, <u>All My Children</u>. She told a young man never to touch a young woman. She hadn't meant the words literally, but he was unable to touch the young woman later. Besides being mentioned and used as a key to healing in this book and my college papers, the concept of specific words having a tremendous impact on people has been unknown in the healing professions' literature, treatment, and practice.

Besides my own experience with these words, during my internship I had an enlightening experience of the burden that these words can create. There was a client in her thirties who had previous psychotherapy. She was missing many building blocks from her childhood. I asked her to tell me what her father had told her she should do. She recited a long list. Then I asked her what her former psychotherapist had told her she should do. This long list went on and on and on for approximately thirty minutes! I told her that she should forget those words, and let mine become important. She heard this with great relief.

Another amazing experience of the power of this new mental structure came to light when I evaluated the results of the short course I had offered to other healers a year previously. A healer suggested I interview a client who had healed dramatically. I asked many questions, and had a tape recorder playing, recording the answers. I asked if the healing partner had said any words of importance to this receiving partner. He said yes.

Gentle Reparenting   The ORIGINAL Guide   J. Alvin

He said that the healing partner had a typed list of statements, and read one to him a week, until all were read.

I asked what these statements were. Then he began to recite the words that seemed important to him that his healing partner said to him over the last year. He spoke the words from his mind. His words matched <u>verbatim</u>, word for word, the typed page of these statements that I had given to the healers in the class I had taught!

He felt that the statements were very naturally helpful. He also felt that being held in the arms of his healing partner was of prime importance in his healing. He believed that attending a 12-step program was of great importance in his healing, as substance abuse was in his background.

The statements that can create new mental structure are not magic words. In receptive clients, a burdensome mental structure from childhood can be replaced by a functional mental structure. These statements will have an impact only if bonding has occurred between the healing partner and the recipient.

However, there is magic in this healing process. But the magic is in the healing power of love shared by the healer and the receiver.

These statements will not always have power. The dependency relationship budding between the healing and receiving partner, the need for bonding on the receiving partner's part, a lovely and safe atmosphere created by the healing partner, good listening, caring responses, holding in arms, feeding, and emotional release of old feelings are all aspects of this healing experience. Add to these the statements that can create new mental structure, and they may or may not have power for this receiving partner at this time. They may not have an impact, at this time, and yet be important at another time. Try offering them, and see.   I suggest that you share this information with the receiving partners, if they are receptive. The more they know, the more helpful they can be in their own healing.

For healing partners, good training is for you to hear these statements from someone who seems nurturing to you. Let yourself feel the impact of the statements that are important for you. Even if they are not significant for you, observe carefully the effect on others for whom they will touch. Develop your sensitivity to the other person's reactions. Notice what they show visually. Do they appear to be opening or closing themselves, are their eyes opening up more, perhaps shining, or are their eyes closing down or growing more dim? What do their bodies seem to be saying? Ask what the receiving partner believes his body to be expressing. Ask if any words had an impact on him.

Following are the statements that can create new mental structure that helped me and others. I gave a copy of these to new receiving partners, and explained that these were temporary statements that help protect people and let them feel safe as they grew and changed. I would offer to say them to the person if they wished, at any time they wished.

Statements That Can Create New Mental Structure:

You should listen to me, and let these words be more important than words from other people, past and present.

You shouldn't kill yourself, or get yourself killed. You shouldn't hurt yourself, or get yourself hurt.

You shouldn't kill anyone else, or get them killed.

Gentleness is the key to your treatment.

You've felt enough pain, you should feel what is safe for you to feel.

Don't withdraw.

Don't run away.

You should remember all that you ever knew, and be able to do the things you need to do (such as drive, shop, cook, work).

I'm glad you are here.

Your needs are okay with me (I'm not afraid of your needs).

Gentle Reparenting   The ORIGINAL Guide   J. Alvin

Your feelings are okay with me (I'm not afraid of your feelings).

I'm glad you're a girl (boy).

You don't have to hurry, you can do things at your own pace.

I like to hold you.

You should ask for what you want, and say what you don't want.

You don't have to take care of me.

Problems are more likely to arise with those receiving partners who have either severe damage from traumas, or great voids in their infant or toddler emotional building blocks. Both the healing and receiving partner should be alert during the twenty-four hours after the receiving partner is given a statement from this list. He may experience discomfort and lose his ability to function. He will know what words are causing him discomfort, if it is the words that are the problem. It could be something else, of course, such as fears or worries or feelings that need to be discussed. It is important for these sensitive and vulnerable receiving partners to have a phone message center available, with a return call within 24 hours, if possible.

To correct the mistakes caused by words, the healing partner can simply say, "Forget the words _____ _____ _____ . For example, if the healing partner said, "Take care of yourself," and those words are causing the discomfort, he can simply say, "Forget the words 'Take good care of yourself'." The exact words are needed, which the receiving partner will know. Within approximately twenty minutes the receiving partner will be relieved of the negative effects of the mistaken statement.

Chapter 7   Emotions, The Atmosphere In Which We Live

"Let me feel what is real, let
me heal what is not, Let me
live each moment coming
straight from my heart.
What I really want is an open heart,
What I really need is an open heart, I
have an endless supply of love in my
heart."

by Scott Kalechstein, from his
album "Midwives of the Light"

We live in an atmosphere created by our emotional state. As adults, we are responsible for our lives. If we do not like the emotional atmosphere we live in, we can change it to one we prefer. I lived in an atmosphere of fear as a child. Then as an adult, I lived in a dreary world where my emotions were blocked. The atmosphere of my life was grey, dreary, depressing, lifeless, joyless, and hopeless.

Like attracts like. When I had many voids within me, I attracted people with many voids. I did not trust anyone. I attracted people to me who also had not learned the lessons of love or trust. They frequently let me down, they were not trustworthy.

When I filled some of the voids from early infancy, I began to feel loved, and I trusted my healing partner. He was the first person I trusted in my whole life. I then attracted trustworthy, loving people to me. As if we have radar, we hone in and attract to us those who have similar emotional and spiritual development to our own.

When I realized that I could change my emotional atmosphere, I decided that I would strive for one of love, joy, pleasure in relationships, and pleasure in my work. It took me years to partially reach my goal, which I still have in front of me. I am still striving for those beautiful goals, and my life keeps getting better, happier, and more full of love and rewards in my work. My relationships continue to improve.

For those of you with fewer missing building blocks and fewer traumas than I had, your healing and growth can be correspondingly quicker, with one condition. I noticed that it is easier for healthier people to heal. But due to the many comforts in their lives because of the many areas of health, healthier people have one disadvantage I never had.

That disadvantage is a complacent lack of motivation to improve their lives. Healthier people need to come up with a good personal reason for a commitment to heal all that they can heal, and not to stop. Then they will have a good enough reason to spend their time and money in healing or personal growth courses.

One way to create a commitment that will help you to grow and continue to grow, is to find a reason beyond yourself. Perhaps you could create a commitment that your family will come together in love instead of being separated, out of your healing. And if you'd like to think globally, even better. The larger your commitment, the more you will grow and heal, and the more you will eventually help others. Maybe you'd like to make a commitment to end world hunger, or create world peace, and you will start by healing yourself so that you are more peaceful and have abundance. It is said that when you have a global commitment, the universe lines up to help you. And you will <u>have</u> to keep growing and healing, in order to give that much to humanity!

My original commitment was to heal for myself. I had years of failure to heal. Then, when I decided to heal in order to give my son a better life, I began to heal. Of course, my son and I both benefitted. Then I decided to make a personal commitment to end world hunger. I didn't do anything other than know in myself that there is enough food for everyone, and that in every way I could, I would help. Later I decided that I would commit to helping heal the planet, and teach love, through my healing method and my writing and speaking. I personally believe that when we are committed to help all of humanity, the spirit world of God gives us extra help.

We reach plateaus after each new surge of growth and healing. We may wish to stay at our new level awhile. Then the road continues to rise in front of us. New growth is always possible, and life keeps getting better, so why stop?

145

What Are Emotions?

Emotions are part of being human. They just <u>are</u>, like the skin on our body and the bones inside. We all have them. We all need them. Emotions are meant to serve us. They are energy. Baruch Spinoza, a philosopher of the 17th century, wrote that "All passions are passages, all emotions are motions, towards or from completeness and power." Spinoza further clarified that by emotions, the power of action in the body and ideas are either increased or diminished.

When we allow an appropriate flow of our emotions, we have all of the energy we need to enjoy our lives and function well. When we block our emotional energy, we often lack energy and the more pleasant emotions, such as love and pleasure.

The basic emotional groups are pleasure, sadness, fear, and anger. We also feel guilt. These all can range from a slight feeling to a great emotional feeling. Sometimes people attempt to block one or more emotion, such as anger or fear or sadness. Unfortunately the other emotions also get blunted, to one degree or another. So when we block feelings we think are less desirable, pleasure gets diminished as well. In fact, we can lose the feelings of pleasure in our life entirely. The good news is that we can gain back our feelings. We can learn to have our feelings serve us. Then we can experience the pleasures that humans are meant to have.

We feel guilt when we know we have done something wrong. Sometimes our mind can concoct feelings of wrong-doing when in fact we have done nothing wrong.

Anger is the feeling that happens when your innocent wishes are blocked. It is not a bad or a negative feeling. Anger provides the energy for you to find a way around whatever is blocking your wish, so that you can get your wish, if possible. So you can see that anger truly has a positive function.

The verbal expression and behavior that you choose when you are angry can be considered positive or negative. Do your relationships suffer due to your expression or lack of expression of anger? If you are one of those people who "never gets angry," perhaps your feeling of anger got blocked long ago. All people have innocent wishes all day long, and sooner or later some will be blocked.

Fear is the feeling caused by actual or threatened danger. We can create unnecessary fear by imagining scenarios of danger in our minds. Sometimes when we are fearful we need information or comforting words from someone. Other times we are scared when we try something totally new. That fear diminishes quickly.

Sadness is the feeling that we feel when we experience loss or emotional hurt. All we need to do to complete our feelings of sadness is to allow ourselves to feel it.

Pleasure is the feeling we have when we receive enough of our innocent wishes. What is enough varies from person to person. To discover what is enough for you, pay attention to how you feel with more or less in a certain area. For example, does going out twice a week with friends satisfy you? Or do you feel better if you are with them only once a week, so that you have time for yourself alone. We can learn balance by paying attention to our emotions and needs, and to what brings us satisfaction.

People with missing building blocks from babyhood and childhood may have difficulty feeling pleasure until they begin filling those unmet needs. Also, people who blunt one feeling or another, usually sadness or fear or anger will feel less pleasure until they allow themselves to feel all of their emotions.

To feel good, we also need contact with other people. Humans are social animals. I consider contact with others "emotional food." This "emotional food" is as necessary to our emotional well-being as food and water is to our physical bodies. When people isolate themselves, they lack this emotional food.

People from very dysfunctional families tend to isolate themselves, and withdraw from the world. In order to heal in this process, it is necessary to find a supportive community to provide "emotional food," so that the healing sessions can fill in the voids from childhood. Working or volunteering a few hours a week, and perhaps taking a class or two, and joining a church or temple are some ways to begin finding kind people to surround you.

Good homework for isolated receiving partners is to find ways to create this supportive community. Assignments to look for classes or work or volunteer opportunities or churches can be given by the healing partner.

To increase your ability to feel your emotions, this type of healing can help, as well as some types of therapy and "bodywork." "Bodywork" is healing directed toward your physical body. Emotional blocks are held in muscles, and can be released by physical touching of the muscles in your body. This may be especially helpful to those who have difficulty accessing emotions in the healing sessions. You can find "bodywork" healers listed in holistic newspapers in health food stores in many areas. Some personal growth workshops such as Life Spring assist people in re-connecting to their feelings.

Unexpressed anger, fear, and sadness can be stored for years in our bodies and minds. Stored "old feelings" can cause energy depletion, because it takes energy to hold those feelings inside. These feelings are meant to be expressed outward, in sound and motion. When that energy is held inside, it can cause stress, and emotional and physical illnesses. These "old feelings" can be expressed in emotional release sessions, described in chapter eight.

What Do Emotions Tell Us?

Our emotions are supposed to serve us. Instead of our emotions serving us, we might be at the mercy of our emotions. Even though we don't want to be fearful, we may be. Even though we don't want to lose our temper at the drop of a hat, we do. Even though we know that life isn't meant to be sad all the time, that's how we feel. Even though our world is dreary because our emotions are blocked, we don't know what to do to feel anything. Even though we are very depressed, we don't seem to get better. These symptoms of emotional distress are all warning signals, like the red light that comes on in our cars when we need more oil, or when our engine is over-heating. These feelings indicate a need for help. You may just need some tinkering by a healing mechanic, or you may need a major overhaul.

Herbs are natural ways to help bring our bodies into balance. They may take a little longer to begin working than drugs, but once they begin working, people feel better than they do on drugs. Herbs are not addictive, and do not have the side effects of drugs. They can be found in many health food stores. Also, practitioners of the Chinese healing arts such as acupuncture are often knowledgeable about herbs.

Emotions are a signal to do something. When the feelings are good, sometimes the only thing needed is to enjoy, and wallow in the good feelings.

Fear is the signal of danger. It serves a survival function. Early man either froze in silence, or ran when frightened. When true danger threatens, those are sometimes the best responses.

Fear also arises in new situations, or in situations that trigger old memories of dangerous events. In these times, you need support from other people. Sometimes an explanation will be all the support you need. Sometimes you need to figure out what you are afraid may happen, and talk over your fears with someone supportive. Sometimes all you need is a friend to accompany you as you try something new.   Sadness is the feeling that comes when we feel hurt or suffer a loss. When we allow the tears to flow, the sadness will leave us after a time. It is most helpful to have a sympathetic listener, and a shoulder to cry on. Crying alone is very painful, and I suggest finding a friend or a healing partner for your sad times. That way your crying is a good cry, rather than unbearable pain.

Grief is the intense sadness from the death of something or someone we hold dear. It may arise from the death of a loved person or pet, or the death of a marriage or friendship. If this grief is expressed, it will eventually wane. In earlier times, widows and widowers wore black for a year. People expected them to be in mourning for that period of time. That was a realistic expectation, as those feelings can ebb and flow strongly for that long.

When the feelings are allowed to be expressed, they will eventually diminish. Support for grief is available, and I suggest that people search for supportive counseling or organizations, rather than trying to handle it on their own. Grief expressed and talked about diminishes. Otherwise it can stay frozen inside, and cause additional misery. There are organizations for widows and widowers, and for parents that lose children, for example.

Anger is a signal that you need to do something to get your wish. You may need to take some time to think about what you need. Think of what you want or don't want. Then you may need to communicate that to someone.

There are many ways to communicate your anger. One way is by screaming at the other person, but this doesn't work very well. People will avoid your company. Another way is to become a silent martyr. This doesn't serve you very well, either. It hurts you to hold such strong energy inside of you, when it is designed to go outward.

Here is a way to communicate anger in a way that has worked well for me, in case you'd like to try it. I call it the "anger sandwich," because the negative is sandwiched in between positives. You can think of it as a club sandwich, with lots of good things on the outside, and a little meat in the center.

First, think of the qualities that you sincerely appreciate in the other person. Then, sandwich what you don't want in between the positive qualities. I usually say two positive qualities first, then mention what I don't like or want, then add two more qualities that I like. I include an expectation that the problem will be solved as one of the positive statements. For example,

+ I love your company, and
+ I love your mellow, easy-going personality.
- I don't want to argue with you anymore, at all.
+ I value your presence in my home, and
+ I appreciate that we always solve our problems.

+ Our friendship has been almost entirely a pleasure,
+ and my goal is to keep it that way.
- We had an upset, possibly a misunderstanding. I'd really like to know if I inadvertently hurt your feelings, or said something that upset you.
+ Something I admire about you is your vulnerability.
+ Another thing I've always appreciated about you is your honesty. Is there anything you'd like to say to me about this, now or later?

If you are not used to talking about your feelings, you may feel scared at first. It gets better with practice. If you are scared to speak up, one way to get started is to start with your feeling of fear, and say, "It's scary, or hard, for me to say this." Or, it's fine to start by writing your communications to the other person.

Speaking up can be difficult as you are beginning to learn this new skill. You can write if you'd like. There are many advantages to written communication. You get to say everything you want, and can plan it well. You can practice as many times as you want before you send it. Your communication won't get interrupted. It is a safe way to communicate. You can put the communication on a beautiful note. The person receiving your note can re-read it, and may even treasure it.

Emotional Problems Are Not Caused By Emotions

Emotional problems are not caused by emotions. Emotions that are a problem are the symptoms. The underlying cause of the problems, from the seriously mentally ill to the fairly healthy person, are missing developmental building blocks and stored "old feelings." That is why filling in missing building blocks and some emotional release work constitutes most of the healing that takes place in this style of healing. Treating the symptoms, now that you know the cause can be treated, is like putting a bandaid on a wound.

155

Innocent Wishes Are Linked To Emotions

All day and night, each of us has a very young inner child that wants what it wants when it wants it. Following is a list of some of the innocent wishes that each of us wants. They are natural desires that cause no harm to anyone. It is important to realize that innocent wishes are normal and common to all humans. These wishes can change from moment to moment. Here are a few innocent wishes:

I want to sleep until I am ready to get up.
I want to eat right now.
I want a drink.
I want to talk and for you to listen to me.
I want to go out for a walk.
I want to take a bath.
I want to wear my favorite shirt.

Here are some more innocent wishes:

touching   being touched
holding someone   being held
being seen being
heard being
acknowledged
talking
listening
seeing
eating
sleeping
playing

spending time with someone
spending time alone
receiving love   giving love
receiving affection   giving affection
being close
hugging*   being hugged*
kissing*   being kissed*
sexual contact*

> Note: the innocent wishes with the stars are only innocent if they are with the consent of both parties. The sexual wishes are only innocent between consenting adults.
> Children are under the age of consent for any sexual contact with adults, and that is always a violation, emotionally and legally.

We do many things to help us gain more of our innocent wishes. We go to movies or to dinner or concerts with friends, to play, talk, listen, and to be close. We earn money so that we can have as many innocent wishes as we desire, a nice home, a car, and to have money to play more.

It is natural for humans to ask for their wishes to be satisfied, and to say what they don't want. We start off asking for our innocent wishes as babies, crying when we have a blocked wish. In healthy families, we are cared for and comforted. As we get older, we learn refinements of asking. We learn that we must share, and wait our turn for some of our wishes. We learn timing, negotiating and waiting.

If we grew up in a fairly healthy family, where many of our needs were satisfied, we comfortably feel all of our emotions. If we have many missing building blocks, we may need to recoup some of them to have open emotional responses.

Notice that both feeling good and feeling angry are linked to our innocent wishes. When we receive our innocent wishes, we feel good. When they are blocked, we feel angry.

There is a range of anger from feeling slightly annoyed to a full-blown rage. The following blocked wishes are the opposite of some of the innocent wishes listed above.

I don't like it that the alarm is ringing now. I want to keep sleeping.

I'm hungry but the cat got into my lunch! It's hot out here, and I'm very thirsty, and there's nothing to drink here.

I hate when you read the paper and tune me out when I want to talk.

How To Help Other People's Anger Disappear

Would you like to know how to help someone's anger disappear? You can! This may take you some practice, but it is worth it. Then when your boss, your spouse, your parents, your child is angry at you, you can be with them in a way that has their anger disappear, and you both can feel good.

When someone is angry at you, what you can do is to <u>really</u> get their points and feelings. To make the anger disappear, you need to receive it with every sense you have, and communicate that you did. It is important to respond non-judgmentally, so use a neutral tone of voice. Sarcasm, criticism or judgement in your voice will sabotage your attempt.

Here's an example. You can fill in any words of anger that fit the ones that come toward you.

You hear, "I am so furious at you ...."
You say, "I get it. I can see how furious you are, and I can hear it in your voice. I really get how mad you are at me."

Then the person continues, "Yes, you ... ... and you ... ... again!"

And you say, "I got it. I ... ... again and I ... ... again, and that's why you are so mad at me!"

And you hear, "And furthermore, ... and ...."

And you say, "I get it. I also ... . and .... , and you are furious about that."

Keep listening to the exact points that the person is angry about, and let them hear that you get how angry they are, that you see and hear their anger, and that you get their points. Continue responding in this way. Soon their anger will disappear! This is useful in all personal relationships, as anger is a part of life. It is also an important skill for the healing partners in this healing process. This type of response to anger honors the other person's feelings and perceptions, with no judgement.

This takes lots of practice to master. You may respond in your habitual way to someone's anger, and then realize that you lost an opportunity to practice. Or you may be trying to listen non-judgmentally, and slipped in your opinion or your judgement or criticism. Or some sarcasm was in your responses. Don't be hard on yourself for being human! You can let it go, and if you are in relationship with this person, if the anger is unresolved, it will come up again.

Or, you can be a very big person, and apologize for not listening, or for not being as sensitive as you'd like. Then you could bring the subject of the person's anger up yourself, and say you'd like to give it another try, and you will do your best to listen to exactly what was upsetting to them. You could even write yourself a little note to coach yourself:

1. hear and reflect feelings
2. hear and reflect points
3. avoid judging
4. keep voice responses neutral

The Power Of Pretend

As humans, we attach meaning to everything. We need to realize that <u>we</u> are the ones who put the meaning on other people's words and actions. Once we realize that we do this, we can examine the meaning, and discover if it is true or pretend.

Here's one example of how we can add our own meaning to an event. The example here is "You look great today!" When someone says this, do we accept it, and feel good? Or do we add a meaning of our own, perhaps one learned from our childhood? Then we don't feel good after receiving the compliment. Maybe we say to ourself, "They are only trying to soften me. They'll want something from me later." Or, maybe we say to ourself, "I do not look good. I look terrible."

If you had a childhood where you received much negative attention, it is a pretty good guess that you re-translate much positive input that comes your way into negative. As a child growing up and leaving a negative childhood, we have great hope that now life will finally be better. But something that all humans do in such childhood situations gets in our way.

That is because we leave a negative childhood with a sort of filter system. We understood our childhood, and had to make sense of it to survive. So we generalized our thinking, that the whole world was like our childhood environment. We did this unconsciously as small children. We then created our personal filter system so that the outside world matched our childhood inner world.

For example, suppose we had 95% negatives in our childhood environment. Even if we are in a 50% positive situation now, we strain 45% of the positive input through our filter, and re-translate it to negative. We attach a personal, made-up negative meaning so that our world feels like the familiar 95% negative world of our childhood. If we could only receive 5% positive as a child, that is how much positive we will trust and allow into our system as adults prior to healing.

This filter system, as I call it, and this re-translating is not conscious. Most people are not aware that they do this unless they are in some sort of group, therapy or personal growth, and hear challenges to their negative thinking from a number of people.

For example, Claire has always thought of herself as ugly and overweight. She is actually attractive and average in weight, but has a distorted view of her physical body due to many missing building blocks in her early childhood. Claire is attending a church potluck. Thomas tells her she looks very nice today. She says, "Oh, I'm just fat and plain. I've always been that way." Thomas says, "Do you really believe that?" She says, "Yes, I accepted it long ago."

Thomas sees Claire's friend Alice, and signals her to come over. She comes, and Thomas says, "Your friend Claire thinks she's fat and plain.

163

Would you tell her what you see?" Alice says, "You are kidding! You are a beautiful woman. I love your eyes and smile. And you aren't fat! Where did you get that idea?"

Claire decides to ask some other friends for feedback. They all tell her in what ways they find her attractive. Claire begins to alter the meaning she attaches to compliments. She now lets more positive in.

There are some sad aspects of this human survival mechanism. First, it is sad that it stays around when it is no longer needed. Second, it is sad that the re-translation people so often do is from positive to negative. We humans can be so hard on ourselves!

It is a good idea to begin to check out negative assumptions. When someone gives you a compliment, and says you look nice, or they like your shirt, try to allow it in without translating it to negative, or lessening the value of the compliment. Try just saying "Thank you." Let the positive attention in.

The re-translating that people do is part of a wonderful ability of our minds. A psychologist named Morris Rapkin called it the "Power of Pretend." It is important for us to realize that first, we have the power to attach meaning to everything. And second, we need to see that as humans, we <u>all</u> attach meaning to <u>everything</u>! When we become aware of this, we then have three choices.

1. First, we can ask the person speaking to us what they mean, and accept what they say as truth. This requires developing the courage to speak up and ask for feedback, and learning to trust.

To test your perceptions, you can get feedback on the same concern from several people . When you hear from five to ten people that their perception differs from yours, and theirs all coincide, you will update your private meaning. This is how you can begin to learn to trust feedback from others. Your old filter system begins to self-destruct.

Also, it may take some development of trust to accept what is said at face value. I personally prefer to accept everything as true unless I have personal knowledge that the person frequently does not tell the truth. I lose nothing by this attitude. I feel good from all compliments, even perhaps a few that may be insincere.

When the information is not complimentary, and is a judgement, I decide whether I want to listen to it. Perhaps it is a gift for my growth, if I am ready. This is not always easy to accept, because my first reaction to criticism is usually defensive. The information is not always given to me in the way I would prefer to hear it. But later, I can quietly think about the comment, and decide to think about it. If I think there is validity to the comment, then I can grow, if I want to. Or, I can set a boundary with that person, and ask them to be with me any time they have something positive to share with me, and to take any negative to their own teachers or healers. Or I may decide it is not correct for me. Then I dismiss it and let it go.

2. A second choice is to continue to pretend the worst. As humans, we tend to do this. For example, someone is late to pick you up. You may think they don't like you, or don't really want to get you. A plane is late, and you worry that it crashed. This is the power of pretend at its most negative. Worry is using the power of pretend. So are negative and judgmental thoughts.

Isn't it interesting how we sometimes excuse our own errors, but have harsh judgements of others? That is because we know our own intentions, and we don't know the intentions of others. If we walked a mile in their shoes, as the old saying goes, perhaps we would be more understanding. We forget this. As humans, we are very quick to judge and criticize others and ourselves.

3. A third choice is to pretend something positive. This is what I do, since I know that as a human I am likely to pretend _something_, so I might as well make up a nice story. If

someone is late, I pretend that they are busy, or caught in traffic, and will arrive soon. Then, when I find out what really happened, I update my mental information. When I start to worry, I catch myself, and pretend something positive. For example, if I notice that my son is late getting home, I will say to myself, I'm not going to worry unless I <u>know</u> something bad happened. I'm not going to pretend bad things. I'm just going to pretend that he's fine, and having a great time, and forgot to look at his watch.

Thoughts generate emotions. Old ideas from our dysfunctional family have another unfortunate contribution to our lives. And don't delude yourself, if you have not been in therapy or personal growth courses you are likely to have most of those old ideas from your childhood. The old ideas trigger old emotional patterns and responses. A brilliant client described this as the old "kit." The old "kit" contains all that we learned in our family. It contains all of the family rules, all of the family version of 'facts' about feelings, thinking, behavior, and the world. The "kit" also contains the family 'pretends,' the stories we tell ourselves when our wishes are not satisfied, and our style of reacting. Our "kit" took years of training to develop.
There are some personal growth and educational seminars that can help us clear our

thinking. One international company that offers a brilliant variety of seminars is Landmark Education.

Phases Of The Healing Process

In <u>Conjoint Family Therapy</u>, Virginia Satir emphasized that "the process still - and always - is the <u>relationship between you and me</u>, <u>here and now</u>." This is true of this type of healing as well. The techniques, the words, the skill of the healer are all within the bonds of relationship between the healing and receiving partners. If the bonding does not begin, this type of healing will not occur.

This healing process is another step in the evolution from the doctor/patient or therapist/client role. It may begin as a doctor/patient or therapist/client relationship; by the end of the process it can be a beloved person to beloved person relationship. The bonds of love can be quite similar to that of a parent and grown child.

In healing sessions in the initial phase, it is very important to note and distinguish the differences between the new situation and the original family situation. A change will occur step by step, as the receiving partner compares old family rules with the new ones in the healing sessions. Besides the areas discussed above regarding 'pretends' and the 'kit,' here are some of the areas he will be noticing regarding problems, solutions, and situations in his life:

1.	the existence of problems, internally or externally
2.	acknowledgement that problems exist, ability to define problems

3. understanding the general possibilities of change, clarifying the significance of problems, able to see and define various options

4. sees personal capacity for change, can come up with solutions, and can select possible choices for action

5. can see his own skills in problem-solving, and chooses options that solve problems

6. knows he can solve problems, and takes action that does solve them.

The above list is in order of growth and healing. It is described in <u>Cathexis Reader</u>, by Jacqui Lee Schiff. The receiving partner will initially be unable to distinguish the lower end of the list until he has learned to understand the top ones. For example, he cannot understand that problems are solvable if he is still operating from his old family system that ignores the existence of problems. He will learn to distinguish in the order above, beginning at number one on the list, if that is the level of his understanding the world from his old family system.

After some time, when his feelings are reflected back to him, and his points are listened to, he will notice how different this is from his childhood experience. He will begin noticing the difference between the "new system" in the healing sessions and his old family system. Here he can talk about his feelings, about what is important to him.

Here he can ask for what he wants, and say "no" to what he does not want. Here, his needs are honored. It is helpful for the healer to point out these differences as the "old family system" and the "new system" in conversations discussing them.

The receiving partner will also be sorting out the difference between three aspects of self-expression. These are emotions, thinking, and rules, values, and opinions.

The first aspect of self-expression are the emotions. They are mad, sad, glad, scared, guilt, and variations of these feelings. It is important for people to clearly state their feelings.

The second aspect of self-expression is the logical, thinking part of us. Like a computer, this part expresses "just the facts, ma'am." Two and two is always four. This is an emotionless, logical part of our mind.

When people mistakenly say, "I feel <u>that</u> ... ... ," such as "I feel that this is the best option for me," they confuse the listener, who is expecting an emotion to follow the word 'feel." When people say, " I feel that ..." they are expressing a thought, not a feeling. For clear communication, this error is best corrected.

The third aspect of self-expression is the part of us with rules, values, and opinions, nurture and criticism. Prejudices are included here. An opinion is a variation of the truth, from that person's perspective. It is important to honor other people's opinions, even if we have an opposite opinion. The other person has formed his opinions based on his life history, which we as listeners cannot perceive. We can ask how they formed that opinion, and perhaps gain some understanding of their perspective. This aspect of the personality will come under much personal scrutiny as the healing process progresses. Old rules and values, opinions and prejudices will die a natural death as building blocks of childhood are filled, as emotional release work is done, as the person becomes more and more open and receptive to other people, and new levels of thinking occur. New values that honor self and others will be consciously chosen.

As an example of this is, Mike had many internal judgements about other people prior to his healing process. He saw much negative around him, and frequently suppressed his internal anger. When asked what he wanted, instead of honoring his own wishes, he submitted to those around him, to be a nice guy. His suppressed anger leaked out, interfering in his life.

Mike began using the charge that he felt from incidents that happened during the week. "My friend was rude. He shouldn't have left the restaurant." He'd lie on a mat and express his feelings of anger toward his friend. The anger inevitably led to early childhood anger at Mike's parents. He expressed that anger during a number of sessions.

After some time, Mike found himself less angry and judgmental with his friends. Then Mike decided that he would speak his truth with his friends. He decided that even if he was angry he would not say or do anything to hurt another person. He created new values for himself.

People sometimes, due to their childhood decisions, limit their self-expression to one or two of these aspects. They often then match up in relationships with people who express what they block. For example, a man who blocks all of his emotions, and expressed criticism and his opinions very strongly may match up with a woman who expresses her emotions frequently. Healing sessions or personal growth courses can help people gain expression in areas that they have closed. Their lives and relationships will grow richer as they express themselves more fully.

It is important that we realize that the decisions that we made as little people in our childhood homes were the best thing we could have done at the time. We cleverly intuited our survival needs, and what would best serve us with our particular parent figures and situation. This is important for healing partners to acknowledge to the receiving partners.

The receiving partners may be very dysfunctional adults now due to those early decisions. But those decisions may have saved their lives, if they came from a violent home! They were good decisions, and necessary at that time. No one could have made better decisions, knowing their situation and their vulnerability. They were wise decisions for their time and place. If I hadn't stopped screaming when my parents pushed me up and down in the bathtub, they might have continued their behavior, and drowned me. Every so often we read in the newspaper of babies and toddlers being killed. So my decision not to feel my emotions was a survival decision, a good decision. It worked. I survived.

In addition, we each are the experts on our own childhood history. We lived it, we interpreted it, it is our story. Other people may perceive our childhood differently, but we were the only one to live it from our own perspective. We have every right to say, "This is how it was for me." It is important for the healing partner to honor the receiving partner's life history. At the beginning of treatment sessions in many forms of healing, the receiving partner relates his problems and perhaps some of his life history, his childhood background. In this type of healing, this initial contact is the first place for the healing partner to begin listening in a way that the receiving partner feels honored and counted, rather than discounted.

The use of the statements that can create a new mental structure can be near the beginning of the process. However, you may wish to wait awhile as you get to know each other. These statements can trigger the receiving partner to enter the childhood stage needed to begin healing his childhood voids. The statements can be offered a few at a time at the beginning of the sessions, until all have been given.

If the receiving partner is functional enough to read and understand, he could read this book. An informed partner is able to be of more help in his own healing.

The phase of returning to childhood experiences can be at any point in this process. For some people, it will be most of the healing, and most of the process. Some will regress and feel like small children. Others will feel like adults playing at being a child, or acting the part. It does not matter. It works either way.

Some receiving partners may come in and simply talk, session after session. They may wish to be held near the end of the session. They may or may not want a bottle, or baby food. They can bring whatever they want to be fed, or the healing partner can have a supply. I did it both ways when I needed healing. Both were fine for me. They may want to talk for a while, then play with children's toys, then get held and fed. They may just want to play.

Emotional release work is an important phase of this healing process. It can come at any time from the beginning of the process to the end. For those receiving partners who were traumatized for expressing their emotions, as I was, it will likely come later in the process. There is no hurry. The pace should always be at the receiving partner's discretion. Doing emotional work should be an

invitation, not a demand. Healing cannot be
coerced.

Persecutor, Rescuer, And Victim, The Drama Triangle

Why is it, when we've done our best to help others, sometimes it is not appreciated and our efforts do not help? Our intentions were good. What happened? We may have entered the drama triangle, discovered by Stephen Karpman, M.D.

When we are asked to help, and we accept, we frequently do help. Everyone ends up feeling better. But when we do not ask if help is wanted, or are not asked for help by the person we want to help, we are interfering. They may not be ready for help, or want help at the moment. If we help when no request for help is present, we enter the drama triangle.

The drama triangle is Rescuer, Persecutor, and Victim. We can step into the triangle from any of the three positions.   Then we will go around to each of the other two positions. So when we help when there is no request, we enter the Rescuer position. We are not appreciated. We then feel like the Victim. "Why don't they appreciate me?" Then we enter the Persecutor position. "Those people just don't know what's good for them."   Other negative, judgmental thoughts follow. We have gone around the whole drama triangle. Dr. Karpman emphasizes that it is the fluidity of the drama triangle that has us move quickly from one position to another, whether we enter from the Persecutor, Rescuer or Victim position.

The person we want to help may be learning a lesson in their muddle. A muddle is what happens when we play in a mud puddle. We get mud all over ourselves. It isn't a bad thing. We learn about that mud puddle. We also learn that we have to clean the mud off afterwards.

We all get in muddles until we learn our lessons. We cannot learn other people's lessons for them. They have to learn them for themselves. There are many lessons to learn. As we get our voids filled, and grow through the childhood stages, we get in fewer and fewer muddles.

Why are we attracted to the drama triangle? We all need attention in order to stay alive. Attention is our "emotional food." Perhaps we have not learned how to get positive attention by making straight requests of others. Or maybe those to whom we make straight requests do not respond the way we wish. We then sometimes choose any attention we can get. Negative attention is better than no attention at all to our wounded inner child.

If we have many missing building blocks from infancy and early childhood, we may be a drama junkie, a term coined by Dr. Karpman. According to Dr. Karpman, the drama triangle is agonizing. It is very stressful. Once we enter into it, our clear thinking deteriorates. Intimacy is lost.

When we get in the drama triangle by being a Rescuer, Persecutor, or Victim, we get ourselves in a muddle! First we become aware of the drama triangle. Next we realize that it is our choice to enter it or not. Then we may choose to get in fewer muddles.

If drama has been our way of life, how can we leave this painful pattern? Dr. Karpman tells of two ways to exit from the drama. The first way is when we see the drama triangle clearly. We may lose our desire for this type of excitement. We may say, "I've had it. I want no more part of it."

Here is the second way Dr. Karpman says we can end this unpleasant excitement in our lives. If we tend to pick the Victim position first, we can say to ourselves, "I'd rather be getting than fretting." We can find a place and people with whom we can make straight requests and receive what we need. If the Persecutor position seems to be our weak spot, we can say, "I'd rather be mad than sad." We can feel the anger of our blocked wishes, and use the energy to leave the poor situation. If we tend to be a Rescuer, we can say, "I'd rather be smarter than martyr." We can think carefully, and find people and places that offer us satisfaction. One of these clever phrases best fits our taste for drama. We can use one of them to help us think rather than act in our old drama pattern.

Some of us love to help others. We would do better to take the best care we can of ourselves, and wait to give help to other adults until it is requested. This is hard for those of us who want to fix everything and heal everyone. However, it is an important lesson to learn.

Healers need to make sure in the healing sessions that the healing is by request. This way the healer remains outside of the drama triangle. The healing partner can wait, and see if the receiving partner makes requests. If no requests are made, you can ask what they would like to do in their session. If they do not know, you can offer choices, would you like to do x, or y, or z today in your time with me, or perhaps something else? Or finally, you can ask if they would like you to make the choice for them. That way the responsibility of choice is with the receiving partner.

There are exceptions. It is sometimes appropriate to be a Rescuer. When someone is suicidal, threatening self or others, or is in a child-like state and extremely upset, these are times to step in when no request is made.

Dr. Karpman says that upon learning of the drama triangle, some people react by never helping anymore. They have then actually moved into the Persecutor position. He says that about 10% of all positions can be entered on purpose as an act of caring. For the Rescuer position, this 10% is a reaching out. 10% of Persecutor is warranted aggressiveness. 10% of Victim is vulnerability.

Dr. Karpman says that when we decide to enter the drama triangle selectively, in that 10% when it is appropriate, we can avoid being the Victim. We can do what we can, and then let it go. We can mentally leave the resulting choices of behavior in the receiving person's hands. What they do with our suggestion or intervention is up to them. For example, Dr. Karpman has a client on Medi-cal. This person was not thinking well, and said that Medi-cal dentists just pull the teeth instead of treating them. This is true, many dentists who treat Medi-cal patients do this. He had three molars that needed repair. He was going to have them pulled. Dr. Karpman looked up the name of a dental clinic that aids people on Medi-cal with treatment. He called his client and gave him the information. He felt this was one of those 10% times to Rescue. Mentally, he decided that whatever action his client took was up to him.

As healing partners, we can point out the positive commitment in the receiving partners' dramas. When the moment is right, we can ask how that positive commitment can be expressed in a way that it will be honored, rather than getting the person in a muddle. Since thinking is poor during the drama itself, this question will be more useful to the receiving partner when they are at least temporarily removed from the drama. When a woman is getting battered by her husband, this is the time for a Rescuer to send her to a shelter. When she is safe, she can think of other ways to express her vulnerability.

Here's an example of the 10% of Rescuer, Persecutor and Victim positions that is beneficial. While at a beach parking lot, I observed a group of young teenage boys shouting their bravado to another group of teenage boys. A fight erupted. I prayed for assistance to be sent. A Rescuer immediately appeared. A large man pulled the boys apart and told them to leave. They began to leave. But then they began to taunt each other again.

The perfect Persecutor appeared. Another man ran over towards the boys, shouting, "Do you want to spend the night in jail? I'll arrest you right now." He began chasing some of the boys, who then fled the area as quickly as they could. The entire incident was over within two minutes.

Requests And Demands

Sometimes people need to learn the difference between a request and a demand. A request implies that a yes or no answer is equally fine. A demand only allows for a "yes" answer. A demand is occasionally appropriate, not often. For example, if someone violated my home with a threat, or something else in violation of my values and what I permit in my home, such as drug use or stealing, I would demand that they leave. There would be no room for negotiation.

If a usually positive and loving friend erupts with criticism and negativity, I set a boundary. The boundary is a demand. There is no room for negotiation. I say, "I need to speak to you and set a boundary. I love the positive moments we share. I will continue to welcome the times when you come to me from a loving place. If you don't like something, please make a request or a suggestion. I will be glad to do the same for you. But I don't want criticism in the way you spoke to me recently. Are you willing to accept my boundary?"

Upon acceptance of my boundaries, one friendship grew and blossomed. The person thought my boundary was good for both of us. He recognized that we both have wounded and very young inner childs. He realized that it helped us both to only meet in a loving space. The door is open for us to do some volunteer work together. When I see him, my heart glows. When he sees me, his eyes shine and his smile stretches from ear to ear.

Another friend turned down my boundary. She was in denial, and ignored most of what I said. She clearly was not available to hear me, so I didn't repeat myself. I said that then our friendship would have to end, and that she wouldn't be welcome in my home or car. She said fine. That was hard for me, and I was upset for awhile. But it was good for me.

Bibliography and Resources:

Scott Kalechstein, poem at beginning from his cassette album, "The Eyes of God," c. 1995, 204 N. El Camino Real, suite 220-E, Encinitas, CA 92024. telephone (619) 492-8726

Stephen B. Karpman,M.D., 4333 California St., San Francisco, CA 94118. Telephone: (415) 221-1234.

Landmark Education. This is a non-profit organization listed in the white pages of major cities all over the world. There are two entry-level courses, and many valuable courses that follow the first courses. Helpful to clarify thinking. Telephones: NY (212) 447-2100 Los Angeles (310) 642-1997

Lifespring, Incorporated. An international organization, helpful for expression of emotions. Telephone: 800-826-4573.

"Anger as a Hot Potato." Voices, Journal of the American Academy of Psychotherapists, 1977, by Maurice Rapkin. This article describes the theory of anger as blocked innocent wishes, and some constructive options for handling it that are used in this healing process.

Cathexis Reader, by Jacqui Lee Schiff, c. 1975, Harper & Row, NY, NY.

Conjoint Family Therapy, by Virginia Satir, c. 1967, Science and Behavior Books, Palo Alto, CA.

The Story of Philosophy, by Will Durant, c. 1926, 1961, Washington Square Press, Simon & Schuster, Inc., NY, NY.

Chapter 8

Advanced Listening Skills

The beautiful relationship needed for this healing process is initiated and completed within the atmosphere created by wonderful listening and observation from the healing partner. My first healing partner's goal in his work was to give his receiving partners' the best hour of their lives in each session. It is a lovely goal that I adopted.

This beautiful goal of his, and his wonderful ability to listen had much to do with my finally beginning to heal with him after failing to heal with so many others. With gentleness, warmth, and patience from the healing partner, the receiving partner can experience each session with the healing partner as the best hour of his life. For someone who has had few good hours in their life, this is a priceless gift.

Special skills in listening are needed to create this atmosphere, and much practice. The benefit of practicing on your friends and family is that those relationships will bloom even more than they already have! Great relationships can become even more profoundly close.

As humans, it is hard for us to listen and observe for long. We have to keep reminding ourselves again and again, continually training ourselves to listen and see and receive more.

In M. Scott Peck's book, <u>The Road Less Traveled</u>, he defines five levels of listening. All of the levels can be appropriate at times, but need to be balanced. The first and worst level is the denial of the need to listen. This is present in homes where children are taught that "children are to be seen and not heard." This refrain was a favorite of my father's. I now talk every chance I get!

The denial of the need to listen is a sad and total abdication of parental responsibility. It is correct at times for all children to learn to be totally quiet, to not distract others. However, it should not be overused, as it was in my childhood.

The second level of listening is to permit chatter but not to listen to it. The person talking is really talking to the walls! If there is a balance of the other levels of listening, this can be fine. Sometimes people just feel like chattering! Again, this is a sad problem if it is the norm, rather than just a part of the picture. My mother chattered, and all of the children chattered. Then she complained that talking to us was like talking to the walls! No one in the family knew how to truly listen.

The next level is pretend listening. If you overdo this with your children, they will grow into teenagers who are <u>expert</u> pretend listeners! They may say, "Uh huh, I understand," in all of the right places, while not hearing a thing! Sometimes people just want closeness, and pretend listening is all that is needed. To discover if this is happening, ask your listeners what they heard you say.

The fourth way that Peck describes is selective listening. This is a variation of pretend listening, with the listener hoping to really listen when something important is said. It doesn't work very well if someone really needs to be heard, but is fine if the person is drifting in and out of communication as they do other things.

The fifth way is what is required to be a healing partner. It is part of the work of committed parents. This is the only true listening. It is to truly concentrate 100% on what the other person is saying. This means to sit down, putting aside chores and personal thoughts, and totally tune in to the other person's thoughts and concerns. It is not a time for talking or advice giving. This is very well described in the book <u>Parent Effectiveness Training</u>, by Dr. Thomas Gordon.

In his book he teaches active listening, to reflect back the condensed meaning and emotions to the other person. This is a crucial skill for this type of listening. It takes practice and it is work.

When I became the healing partner and wanted to give the gift of listening, I really had to stretch myself. It was so healing for me to receive the gift of truly being heard. It was then worth it to me to work hard at giving the gift of listening to others in need of this healing. It is also a lovely gift to give friends.

True listening is a choice. Sometimes I forgot that, and was a true listener to my friends for many years. Then I realized that I was on automatic pilot, and not choosing when to listen if I did it all of the time. So now I don't always listen in this intense, concentrated way. I choose when and with whom I will truly listen.

It is important to remember that all forms of listening are loving responses, if there is a balance. True listening is needed when someone has strong or deep feelings to share. When the feelings of anger, fear, and sadness have been shared and totally received, you may be blessed by hearing deep feelings of love and closeness.

Giving love to another involves more than just feeling the love, or expressing that feeling. True listening is the <u>work</u> of love. It takes a giving of our time and giving our entire attention to another. At first it is hard, and it may always be hard. We all like to think of ourselves and our own concerns. Do not feel bad about this. It is not wrong, nor are you wrong for thinking of yourself. It is just part of the condition of being a human being. Our minds are made to do this.

The chatter and conversations in our brain go non-stop in our waking hours. When we haven't trained our mind, it tends to wander like a small child. So true listening takes work and mind-training.

Rewards will come. You will be rewarded by the growth and glow you see in the person to whom you truly listen. You will also learn from them. Children, parents, spouses, friends and clients can be very wise.

Also, the true listener will grow as a person. You will find yourself extending yourself out of caring for the person you are hearing, whether it is your child, your spouse, or someone you are healing. Once your mind is stretched, it doesn't go back to it's original size!

Sometimes we think we are truly listening, and are unintentionally pretend listening. Here are some clues that point to this all too frequent human error, gleaned from a wonderful book for healers, Holistic Nursing:

1. Being quiet as you think of what you will say next
2. Listening so you will be listened to in return
3. Trying to listen selectively
4. Pretending to be interested when you truly are not
5. Listening selectively or pretending to listen so that you don't disappoint the other person
6. Listening so that you will avoid the chance of rejection
7. Listening for weaknesses to later exploit for self advantage
8. Finding flaws in order to have a more powerful reply

These healers point out that the first focus of listening is to find out <u>what is happening</u> with the other person, and the second focus is to <u>let it be</u>.

Another area to listen for is the positive background commitment of the speaker. What is unspoken, yet in the background? For example, Sheila complains about the horrible way her boss speaks to her. He is very critical. She also speaks of the long hours she works, the detailed reports she is creating, and the good job she does.

The healing partner could point out that unspoken, yet in the background is Sheila's commitment to excellence, and that it seems that she is committed to excellence in her work and in her relationship to her boss. This is a way of honoring the highest and best in Sheila, as she expresses her humanness in her dealings with her boss and her wishes to be spoken to in a way that honors her.

Sheila also complains about her father's constant harping at her to keep her nose to the grindstone. He calls her and criticizes her for going out to classes. He tells her that her interest in martial arts is not ladylike.

She learns that she can thank her father for his commitment to her success in life, and to her well-being. However, in her emotional release sessions, she screams at him in fantasy and tells him to stop talking to her that way. She frees herself of the "charge" that his words trigger in her.

She could actually tell her father the specifics that bother her in her conversations with him. But how likely is he to change his way of speaking? She could set limits on the conversations with him. But she tries speaking to his positive background commitment first. Their relationship shifts, and becomes more positive. Her father feels heard and appreciated, and stops criticizing her. Speaking to a person's positive background commitment is a very powerful way to relate to people.

To train myself to truly listen as I became a co-healer, I sat in sessions with my finger over my mouth to remind myself to only listen! I was so tempted to make suggestions and give advice. I later learned to hold those thoughts for the end of the session. If it was appropriate, I would then ask the receiving person if they wanted to hear my suggestion as a possibility. If they did not want to hear it, I let it go.

Many of the people in need of building blocks in early stages of development never experienced respect for their opinion, their needs, or their pace. It is extremely important to respect their boundaries, so that they can learn to respect their own boundaries. It is an intrusion of their boundaries to make suggestions or give advice if it is not requested.

Practice For Intimacy

We are not intimate just because we have lived with someone for years. In order to be close with someone, we must disclose our true feelings and thinking. This exposure of our inner self takes courage.

Speaking from our inner self, our feelings and wishes and thoughts, is a learned skill. A safe way to practice speaking from your feelings is to be alone in your home, or in a healing session, and pretend that someone you need to talk to is sitting in an empty chair, or is represented by a pillow. If you have difficulty starting to speak, look at the place where you imagine the person to be, and say, as if they were there, "It is hard for me to speak about my feelings to you."

Continue to speak to the fantasy person in the present tense. Rather than saying, "I hate that you spoke to me in that tone of voice. I hate that you read the paper this morning instead of talking to me," which is past, say "I hate that you speak to me in that tone of voice, I hate that you read the paper instead of talking to me," as if it were happening now.

Emotional release work as described below is practice for intimacy. The advantage of speaking from your feelings in a healing session rather than by yourself is that you have a coach with you, to encourage you. Ideally, you also have the feeling that the healing partner is on your side, and understands your feelings and point of view.

Healing With Emotional Release

Emotional release work actually begins during the receiving partner's initial contact with the healing partner. As the reasons for coming for healing are disclosed, perhaps as the life history is told, an atmosphere is created by the healing partner's reception of the healing partner.

In later sessions, as the receiving partner who is unaware of his feelings talks in a deadpan voice about a horror story, the healing partner can point out that the person's eyes are moist. He can ask if the person feels sad about the event being described.

A receiving partner who feels without much thinking will learn in later sessions that she can cry if she wants, or ask for help, or stop and think what she needs. Sometimes people need to learn the difference between old feelings that can be released and current feelings that are a signal to do something and solve a problem.

In the ongoing sessions, these hints of feelings under the surface can be gently pointed out. "You drew your body in as you told me that. What were you feeling?" If the person is unaware of the feeling, the healing partner can say how they looked. "You looked scared as you pulled into yourself just then." Or, "You have tears in your eyes as you speak of that. Are you feeling sad?"

People whose emotions are totally blocked will then begin their emotional work. That is the work of beginning to allow themselves to feel their emotions, and learning the names of the feelings. Prior to my healing experience, I used all the words for feelings that other people did. I didn't have any idea that other people felt their feelings, while I only felt pressure and more pressure, hot and cold, and pain. When I began to feel my emotions, they were strange sensations. I had entered a new world that looked the same as it always had, but <u>felt</u> different. It was like being on a new planet, a twin earth! I had to learn to think all over again with feelings, as well as learning the names of these new sensations.

At some point in the healing process, the receiving partner will be ready to release old feelings from childhood. I was not able to do this at all in the first year I was healing, and then released feelings in a general way for another two years. Only after several years, as I gained more building blocks within, was I able to actually speak directly to the fantasy of my parents in healing sessions far removed from them in time and space, and allow the strong feelings of sadness, hurt and anger to emerge.

The dynamics of each healing session are charge, discharge, nurture, relaxation. The charge can be transformed into discharge by talking or doing emotional release, or both. Then the person is held and fed, if wanted. Afterwards there can be a period of relaxation, a short rest.

Releasing feelings is a learned skill. It helps to have someone sitting quietly nearby, who will be supportive yet not interfere. That takes training on the part of the healing partner. Too much or too little input can get in the way of feelings being expressed.

Good training for healers is to do emotional release sessions, followed by being held, for themselves. It is a good idea to do them at least once a week for a while. You will gain practice looking for areas of "charge" to begin your sessions. You will learn what you need to do to permit your feelings to emerge. This will help you become sensitive to your receiving partners' needs when they do this work.

People who don't feel their emotions may be able to close their eyes and notice the sensation in their bodies. They may become aware of an area that has sensations, such as their stomach or their throat. They can be encouraged to say a word or a sound from the location of the sensation. If they say that they don't know of a sound or word, you can suggest that they focus on the sensation, and softly and repetitively say, "Oh," or "No." The feelings and words may come. If they don't, then reassure the person that when the time is right, and they are ready to feel their feelings, the feelings will come. Remind them that there is no hurry. They will heal and feel at their own pace, and that their body has great wisdom in knowing <u>their</u> timing.

Someone very repressed emotionally may benefit by standing in a corner of the room and shouting, "hey" a number of times to the other corner of the room.

When feelings are blocked or repressed, sound is also repressed. Making sounds can open the door to feelings.

Some receiving partners need nothing but the quiet presence of a healing partner. They lie down on a soft mat, and out come the tears and the words.

Others need coaching and direction. For example, Sheila lies down on the mat. She may, for example, want to work on her anger at her boss for his way of speaking to her. Have her fantasize her boss at some point above her on the ceiling, and speak to him in the present tense. Tell people who are expressing anger to keep their eyes open so they don't get a headache.

She may say that it's hard to know what to say, or how to start. Tell her to say _that_ to him. That may be enough coaching, and she may continue on her own. If she stops, you can suggest she tell him what she does not like (her blocked wishes). As she tells him what she does not like, look for her expression of feelings. You may hear anger in her voice, and then can say, "Tell him that you are angry. Let him hear it!" Or you may see tears and a sad look. You can say, "you look sad."

When you notice the feelings, that gives her permission to notice them. She may cry at this point. When she stops, you can quietly ask what the sadness is. Many things can happen at this point. That may be all that is safe for her to feel, and it is time to stop this part of the session. Or, for someone comfortable with their feelings, this may be a reminder of something sad in childhood. Then they can be directed to speak to that childhood person, if they wish.

When the person makes comments about their feelings, keep coaching them to say it to the fantasized person. For example, Sheila says that she feels hurt that her boss speaks to her the way he does. The healing partner tells Sheila, "say that to <u>him</u>." She says it to him, and stops talking, and some tears come to her eyes. "Say it to him again." This can be repeated until the feelings are not forthcoming.

Then the coaching could be " Tell him not to speak to you that way." Sheila says this in a sad voice. "Tell it to him like you mean it." Now Sheila's voice gets stronger, and anger comes through. She stops again. "Tell him that you are angry!" is the coaching, in a louder, angry voice, modeling the expression of anger.

Sheila says, "I'm mad at you. And I'm mad at my dad who was just like you. I hate you both!" If she stops, say "Say it again," and hit the mat with your fists as you say it, "like this." A quick demo from the coach, "I hate you (smack), I hate you (smack), I hate you (smack)" Then as Sheila begins, and gets wound up, encourage her in an excited voice, just after she speaks, "That's right, let him hear it!"

Most strong feelings eventually lead back to the main caretakers of childhood. Sheila, who is comfortable with expressing feelings, may easily switch from dealing with her boss to talking in fantasy to a parent figure. Other people may not be ready.

During the talks at the beginning of sessions, the healing partner can point out that certain things they discuss seem to have more of a "charge" than others. The receiving partner can begin to take note of those times, and use the "charged" area as a tool to do emotional release work. The receiving partner begins to view these uncomfortable, heightened feelings in a new way. Instead of perceiving these feelings as something awful to get rid of, these "charged" feelings are now seen as a tool to his healing.

In addition, the receiving partner can be asked at what other time in the past he remembers feeling the same way. For example, Mary is sad about the rejection of another friend. She keeps people at a distance by creating disharmony, and has a pattern of making and then losing friends. She has expressed her sadness about that. Asked when she felt that feeling before, she begins sobbing, as she remembers feeling that way when her grandmother died when she was eight. Depending on her readiness to feel her emotions, that may be enough emotional release for the session. However, Mary wants to work further with these feelings. She lies on the mat and says all of the things to her grandmother that she needs to say. Many tears come, as her feelings come. Coaching and encouragement for sad feelings can be in a soft voice.

Feelings come in waves. Mary may feel waves of sadness and grief, followed by waves of anger that her grandmother left her. She may complete everything she needs to say in one session, or may take several sessions to complete expressing these feelings.

Sophisticated receiving partners who are very comfortable with their feelings may enter the session ready to do emotional release work. They may say that they noticed that they had a lot of "charge" while speaking to someone a few days before, and be ready to do emotional work with no further talk. They may be able to direct themselves by then, and only need the quiet support of someone by their side. They lie down on the mat, and begin speaking to someone in fantasy, and the feelings come.

Each person will know when he is through expressing feelings for that session. Honor that knowledge, and end this part of the session.

Crying alone can be very painful. Crying with an active listener, perhaps crying on the shoulder of someone, is a very nice release. It is a relief to let the tears flow, and a mental relief to feel that someone understands your feelings and perceptions. It actually can feel good to cry when you are lovingly received.

It is very important that emotional release is not pushed. When the person is ready, and the environment correct for that receiving partner at that time, the feelings will come. Each person's timing and pace needs to be honored.

Those receiving partners with early unmet needs will benefit by being held and, if they want, fed a baby bottle after the emotional release. Everyone, even if there are few unmet needs, will enjoy the nurture of being held after emotional release.

Emotional release followed by holding sets a pattern of safety. As time goes on, more feelings are opened and released, as the experience of crying or yelling, and then being held quietly become familiar.

One woman explained how being held after working with her feelings made feeling more in the next sessions safer and safer. She said, "When you were holding me, that's when I felt safe to let go of my feelings more. I mean, there's just something in my kinesthetic system that wouldn't be reached by talking... ."

She spoke of other emotional release work without the holding afterwards. She would be angry in the sessions, and then she would stay angry all week. She said, "Yeah, afterwards that was.... yeah, that was important, afterwards, too. To have comfort, and you'd give me plenty of time that you'd just hold me and I really relaxed, and then I wasn't carrying over a bunch of stuff during the week."

She continued, "I could feel you accepting me. I mean it's one thing for somebody to tell me, 'I'm fine with you, I accept you,' and even if they said it to me in an effective way, but that doesn't reach my kinesthetic system like holding does. It's just that system needs that kind of contact for me and I think for a lot of people, too."

After emotions are released, the person is very open and vulnerable. They are especially receptive at this time to the warmth and close contact with the healing partner. It is a good idea for the healing partner to be quietly responsive at this time. The receiving partner may simply relish the quiet and calm after the strong emotional release. Or she may have some questions or share some insights. It is not a time for more than just simple answers and acknowledgement of what is spoken.

A word of warning here: the receiving partner may be especially open to the words of the healing partner at this time. I suggest that it is better to err on the side of too few words rather than too many, and to say no "should" statements except those on the list in chapter seven. Being quiet and listening responsively is the safest route!

My first healing partner ended my session in a way that I loved. After emotional release, holding and feeding, he got up, and quietly covered me with a light blanket, and left the room for a while. I experienced this as a safe nap, lovingly attended. When I was in my childhood state, I asked him not to leave the room. He graciously complied. We later did this with other receiving partners. We usually left the room for five to ten minutes, while the receiving partners rested.

We would then return to the room, and ask how the person was feeling. The answer was always positive. We would then quietly talk for a very few minutes about the session, or homework, and end the session.

Bibliography:

Parent Effectiveness Training, by Dr. Thomas Gordon

Holistic Nursing, by Dossey, Keegan, Guzzetta, and Kolkmeier, c. 1995, Aspen Publishers, Gaithersburg, Maryland.

Chapter 9

Responsibilities Of The Receiving Partner

Safety Guidelines For Receiving Partners To Select Healing Partners

It is important for you, the receiving partner, to know that <u>you</u> are responsible for the selection of the best healing partner for yourself that you can find. You may discover that the one you have chosen is not responsive to you, and it is a struggle for you to get heard, or to get your young child needs attended. It is your responsibility to change to another healing partner. Leaving a healing partner can be very difficult for people with unmet needs in infancy and early childhood. Here are a couple of suggestions of ways to handle it.

One way is to talk this over with your healing partner, and say goodbye. If this works for you, this is the best option.

If you are very dependent on the present healing partner, here is another way. You can look around for another healing partner while you are still with your present one. Then you can begin sessions with the new healing partner, still seeing the old one for a while. When you feel safe letting go of the old healing partner, then you can say goodbye to that person. This is fine for you to do. Your healing partner may or may not agree with your choice, or this way of handling it, but you have every right to make a change, and make the transition in a way that works for you.

If you find that saying goodbye to the present healing partner becomes a struggle, another way may be your best option. You can send the present healing partner a letter or postcard stating that you have decided to stop seeing them. You do not need to give a reason unless you want to.

Now let's say you are with a healing partner that seems to be a good match for you. What are your responsibilities?

You are responsible for your feelings. No one can make you feel anything. Because of your life, you may have touchy areas, and may have strong reactions when one of those spots gets touched even symbolically. Still, that is <u>your</u> reaction and <u>your</u> feelings. You may lack skills in handling your feelings. You can gain those skills as you heal.

You are responsible for your behavior, both in the healing sessions and in the rest of your life. You make choices in how to behave. Then you live with the results of your choices. If you do not like the result, you can make another choice.

If you are in a crisis, it is your responsibility to call for help. If your healing partner cannot or will not help, call a mental health hotline, or a mental health professional who will help. If your life or someone else's well-being is in danger, call the police.

When you are selecting a healing partner, notice if the person listens attentively. If it is very difficult for you to judge, it may be wise to begin healing sessions on a trial basis. Then you can have more time to notice if the healing partner seems warm and attentive, and is a good listener. If you are hearing a lot of "shoulds," this healing partner will not be appropriate for this healing method.

Ask the healing partner in your interview if they would be willing to hold you and feed you, and let you be "little," to act as a young child, during the healing sessions.

Ask the healing partner if they guide people in emotional release work. This is an important skill for this healing method.   Those who do not guide people in emotional release work may simply be untrained. However, this also might be a healer who is not comfortable with emotions. For this healing method, it is best to find a healing partner who is comfortable with emotions.

You may find a healing partner who has never done this type of healing before. Few healers have, at this point in time. However, if they are good listeners, and are comfortable with feelings, they may be willing to give this a try with you. That is how it was with me and my first healer. Sometimes no training can be an advantage, because many healers in this culture are trained not to touch you, and not to allow you to become dependent. Both being held and being allowed to become dependent are necessary ingredients for this healing method.

Both of you could use this book as a guide, if the healing partner is willing.

Even if your healing partner is not willing to read this, you have, and you can steer your process by your requests, and figure out what is happening on your healing path by using this book as a guide. My healing partner did not like to read, so my requests were the triggering factors. It worked for a while, with great benefit to me. Then I had to find a new healing partner for more work.

That also worked for a while, then I had to find new healing partners again to complete my healing. I am still in the process of healing, and will be able to completely fill my remaining building blocks with my present healers.

Even though leaving each healing partner was <u>very</u> difficult, I retained the gains I made with each one. When I was ready, I found my next healing partner.

Safety Guidelines For Healing Partners, Limits To Set

One of the most important discoveries for the healing partner is his or her own limits. You need to decide whether you want the relatively easy and pleasant task of helping fairly healthy people fill in their missing building blocks and do emotional release work. You need to decide how much of your life you are willing to give to others, and then set limits by your working hours and your availability by telephone.

Healing the healthier receiving partners is generally a shorter term process than healing those with great missing building blocks in infancy and very early childhood. That is an important factor for your consideration.

In addition, the healthier receiving partners may be sensitive, and tell you just when you make mistakes. But they won't have the fragility of the people who are missing major building blocks in infancy and very early childhood. These may be good people with whom to practice and to learn the basics   before you attempt to heal someone with a greater need.

If you are working in a office or a home, you may wish to limit yourself to those with enough self-control to never threaten violence, either to themselves or others.

In addition, those receiving partners with substance abuse problems need to have been in a recovery program such as AA for a year. They need to have taken responsibility for being drug-free for some time for this process to be effective for them.

Those healing partners working in facilities such as hospitals or residential and related out-patient treatment facilities may already have training and techniques to deal with violent or other out of control behavior. This healing method could be adapted to many existing treatment plans.

If you wish to use this process with the chronically mentally ill, or for people with great gaps in their infancy or very early childhood development, expect this to be a longer-term process. Your skills and ability to listen and receive the person will need to be more highly developed than is needed to help healthier people heal.

The fears that these receiving partners must overcome will be greater. They will be scared to death, whereas healthier people are just scared. They actually will have terrors rather than fears.

Their lack of trust is a barrier that will need to be overcome. This may take time, many questions, and testing.

These needier receiving partners may be ultra-sensitive to every conceivable error on your part. This means extra time is spent listening and correcting yourself and comforting this person with a fragile and very young inner child.

There are many more building blocks to fill than with healthier people. More time and greater patience will be required to work with these receiving partners. Individual sessions may be welcomed by these receiving partners when they become ready to be held and fed, or to "be little." After they fill in some of the building blocks of infancy, they may wish to be in a group with others.

Some healing partners may offer these types of healing experiences in a group setting. For the healthier population, those who are functioning in the world of work and who are in relationships, group processes will be very effective.

It is important not to add too many rules to the list of temporary "shoulds" that constitute the creation of the new mental structure. It is important not to add more "shoulds" of your own.

Here are some important questions for healers to answer before you decide to do this healing process with people.

> Do you have an ability to trust other people?
> Do you feel loved by the significant people in your life? Do you have significant people in your life?
> Are you comfortable with your own and other people's emotions?
> Are you kind to people even if you are angry?
> Do you keep your word?

If you answered no to any of these questions, you are not ready to offer this type of healing to others. I suggest you become a receiving partner, and fill in your early voids. Then you will answer 'yes' to these questions, and your own healing will be great training, as well.

Can you hear criticism in a non-defensive way? Can you admit your mistakes? Will you always be willing to look objectively at yourself, and admit to your shortcomings? This will be needed to be a healing partner with this method.

Do you permit yourself to cry when you are sad, feel scared when appropriate, feel angry at times, and guilt when you know you have done wrong? Do you have skills to speak to others about your feelings and have a positive outcome to your communication?

Are you good at balancing your life, and making sure that you have enough rest and relaxation, and time for fun? A workaholic healer may need to fill in some building blocks, do some emotional work, and balance his own life before offering this healing method.

The Safe Use Of Personal Power

It is possible to allow people to become dependent on you without victimizing them. This will take a careful monitoring of yourself.

Are you doing this to feel good about yourself and feel more powerful than those you assist, or are you doing this to create and learn from each receiving partner?

If your intentions are clear, and you decide to offer this type of healing, you are in for a great learning experience. You will also be receiving some very unique and beautiful rewards. You will be providing the foundation for others to bloom and have a great life. God bless and guide you!

Barriers For Healing Partners To Overcome

As I said in the beginning of this book, there are many roads to Rome. People find healing and growth in education, religion, psychotherapy, in many areas of life. This healing process can fit into these varied expressions of human growth, if human-imposed barriers are dropped and limits are expanded.

Most adults will have an initial barrier to overcome to hold and feed adults as if they were small babies and children. However, this will disappear quickly as they experience it themselves, or begin to offer it. You will be surprised to find the strong maternal and paternal feelings that arise within you as you do this.

Fulfillment of early childhood needs is not frequently directed to adults, but is often offered to young children. Highly trained people offer care in nursery schools, pre-schools and day-care homes. The boundaries of <u>who</u> can receive this care could be expanded to include adults and older children.

The boundaries of <u>who</u> can offer healing must expand. Mental health professionals dedicate their lives to healing. But there are not enough of them to reverse the famine of the heart, due to the enormous level of need in our culture.

The boundaries of <u>where</u> this could be offered could expand to schools, workplaces, and many other locations.

This could be offered as a psychotherapy treatment. Many mental health professionals are already highly trained in some of the elements of this healing. Mental health professionals are trained not to touch clients, and not to encourage dependency. These barriers must be overcome.

As in any method for improving mental health, it is best to experience this yourself at least briefly before offering it to others. For many clients, this can be offered in the healer's normal time arrangements of a weekly or twice-weekly individual session, or in groups.

For healers in religious-based organizations, you may have similar barriers as the mental health professionals. You have likely been trained not to touch, and to discourage dependency. You may have been trained to leave all healing in God's hands. Whose hands do you think yours are? God has many ways of healing. Here is one more way.

You will need to find a way of seeing that all emotions are acceptable in the healing sessions for the young inner child of the receiving partner, even, for example, if you teach the adults in your services to avoid fear and anger.

Remember that a toddler's experience of God will be different from that of an adolescent, which will be different from an adult's. Adults experiencing this healing may discover a different relationship to God in each different stage of development that they explore.

Chapter 10

Spiritual Growth

Emotional and spiritual growth does not change the fundamental truth of your being. Unneeded protective barriers that you cannot see, but others frequently can, begin to disappear. This growth lets the lost and beautiful 'real' you emerge, as you begin to express more and more of your true self. The 'unreal' you gets chipped off. It is said that Michelangelo was asked how he carved the beautiful statue of David from a slab of marble. He replied that he just chipped away all of the marble that wasn't David. That is what spiritual and emotional growth does for you.

You only leave behind the masks and barriers and the pieces of 'not you' that you stuck on here and there. The more you know your true self, the more you will love yourself and others. As Sujata says in <u>Beginning To See</u>, "when you find out who you really are, it's beautiful beyond your dreams."

As the real you emerges, your true gifts will unfold. You will discover the unique contribution that only you can give to the world. Honor yourself. If your true self and your gifts seem deeply buried, remember that great treasures often take a heroic quest to discover them.

If you seek and persevere, you will find your way. Remember that you are the one who buried your treasures. Within you are the keys to unlocking the barricades and closed doors that you built. After all, you created them!

Search for the healers or personal growth courses or spiritual learning that attracts you. You might ask for God's help in your quest, and if you have no belief in a higher power, you might ask, "If there is a God, or higher power, let me become aware of it." Enjoy your journey. Bon voyage!

What Is Love?

Love has been the subject of philosophical inquiry since man has been able to think and reflect and question. It is the founding cornerstone of all of the major religions of the world. It is the uniting energy in families and friendships. It furthers procreation of the species. It is what inspiring songs say that we need. But what is love, and how can we receive more love?

I am going to describe my experience of what love has been to me in various stages of my life, and then share some of my research with you. As I have been on a quest for love since I was a young child, I have discovered more and more regarding love as time and my probing and searching have continued. I am certain that I have much, much more to discover.

As a young child, I was aware by the age of 11 that love was almost entirely missing in my life, other than a slight sense of love from my father, and in the melting feelings I felt when I was the recipient of the rare kind acts or words from people outside of my family. I remember searching the adult sections of the library, and finding a book called, "Keys to Happiness."

I call that sense that love is missing "the voids within." As I began to heal with my first healing partner, I discovered that I, in conjunction with him, could re-create the experiences that infants and children in loving homes take for granted as a

218

birthright. I first began to feel the warm feeling in my body as I was held as a small child might feel when being held by a warm and loving person.

The adult in me retreated, and the small infant and child within me came forward. I discovered what love is to a baby, even though I was 33 years old! Love to a baby is being held in warm arms, being fed when needed, and bonding closely to a warm man and woman.

Love varies in the six stages of childhood. Love for toddlers is developing a sense of independence within safe limits, unconditional acceptance of the person with limits set on behavior. Love of the world outside of the self begins with an exploration of everything in sight, sound, touch, taste and smell.

Love to the child of 18 months to three years is answers to all the "why" questions with honesty and reasons, and time spent with those warm parent figures. From ages three to six, love is a safe return to nurture after forays with people and experiences away from the parent figures. Love for a six to twelve year old child is the wide wonderful world of things to do and rules to discover and test, with a continuation of the home base of nurture.

Love to an adolescent is an attempt to fill any voids from the previous five stages of development. Loving feelings with new elements surface, as romantic ideas and erotic sensations arise. A wide range of experiences shared with loving, informative

219

adults help develop the intellect. Love for the older adolescent is a safe transition to an independent life.

In the book <u>Care of the Soul</u>, Thomas Moore addresses one of the voids common in people. It is the soul's longing for closeness with God. In his book he teaches the "care of the soul" and an acceptance of lifes ups and downs as lessons to ponder and learn.

Although some of my spiritual beliefs are probably different than yours, the simple core beliefs are the same in all the major religions. If you do not resonate with the thoughts I share, put them aside, and look for areas that are useful to you.

In the <u>Gospel Revealed Anew by Jesus</u>, a book written in the early part of this century, Jesus came through in automatic writing. In this book, Jesus teaches that our soul is constructed to long for closeness with God. He teaches that we must ask for this love to fill our soul. He makes a distinction between the natural love that God has given us to make life on earth tolerable, and is a wonderful gift in itself, and this other love from God, which he calls Divine Love. He teaches throughout the four volumes of the book that this Divine Love is a greater law than the law of compensation, which is the law of cause and effect. The law of compensation is where "we reap what we sow," meaning that our good actions and positive, loving thoughts bring the positive acts and thoughts back to us, while our negative behavior and thoughts brings the same to us.

Gentle Reparenting   The ORIGINAL Guide   J. Alvin

According to these books, when the Divine love begins more and more to fill our hearts and souls, by our daily requests, our soul changes in substance. As this Divine Love progressively fills us, more and more of our errors are no longer a part of us, and we therefore can progress much more rapidly in our spiritual growth than by the slower process of purification that occurs after each earth life as we repent of the harms we have done. The Divine Love removes the cause, and the law of compensation has nothing to act on.

When I learned Spanish and French, I discovered that love is expressed more easily and frequently in those languages. Our English speaking culture tends to emphasize the thinking part of our personality development, while the French and Spanish speaking cultures include more of the feeling aspects of the personality.

In a channeled book, <u>Mary's Message to the World</u>, Mary, the mother of Jesus, speaks about the inadequacy of the expression of love in the English language, with only one word for love. She says that the English speaking people do not understand the importance nor the effects of love in everything we do.

I will describe the types of love that Mary describes so beautifully. When more of the building blocks of childhood are filled in a person, they will experience more of many kinds of love. Those who received less love as a child will be able to experience less of the love that Mary describes.

Mary speaks first of general love. This love is seen in friendliness and respectful regard for all life, people, plants, and the earth. It is a sense of connection with all of the life surrounding us. It is the bonding glue of friendships and matrimony. It helps us remain in relationship in difficult times.

Next Mary speaks of appreciation. Love is expressed through our appreciation of the little and the common surrounding us, and the wonderful and unique creation that we each are. She teaches us to show appreciation to the objects around us, such as our car and home, by the care we give. She says that inanimate objects function better when we talk to them in our mind, surrounding them with appreciation. She tells us to appreciate our wondrous bodies that can sense the outside world with our five senses, and our inner world with our incredible minds. She tells us to appreciate all people, the changing seasons, the common ground we have with all people, even our enemies.

Then Mary speaks of romantic love. She says that it is a glimpse of Divine Love. In our human expression of romantic love, it is a conditional love that says "I will love you _if_..." She says romance is good for a marriage, however, we should know that it is an illusionary feeling. A setting, a poem, or the words of a song can evoke it. She says that it is the wonder of love that we need in marriages.

She tells of the mature love that a parent has for a child, an owner for a business or possessions. With mature love comes responsibility. This is the

love that is given without thought of return. It is
love that sees the defects in others and loves in spite
of or even because of them. I say that this is an
aspect of Divine Love that we receive from God
and our spiritual teachers, guides, and angels.

Then Mary speaks of unconditional love.
This is the love toward children and our life
partners. It is the love God has for us. With this
love, there is no condition, no "if," no action
needed, no rules to be followed.   Divine love heals
broken bones, broken homes, broken spirits and
broken personalities. She says that love is alive, and
grows as it is given to others.

Mary teaches of love as energy, faster than the
speed of light. She speaks of love as chemistry, an
energy source as we know light and electricity to be.
She says that love is the agent that makes our blood
cells move around in our body, that runs our world
and the entire universe.

In <u>Beginning to See</u>, Sujata teaches people to
begin to love by beginning to love oneself more. He
says to reflect first on our own good qualities and
kind acts. When loving thoughts towards ourself
flow freely, we then can extend these thoughts to all
other beings.

Love is a lesson that many of us come
to learn in our lives. We choose various situations in
order to learn to give and receive love. I chose
abusive parents, and on a very long and difficult
path, learned to love, and then gave my parents and
other family members my unconditional love. I am

rewarded with loving relationships where they did not exist before, and am being rewarded by gifts from my spirit teachers for learning this lesson and giving this love.

Spirit teachers, guides and angels are those instruments of God who help us live our lives. I became acquainted with mine in the last couple of years. My Buddhist Priest teacher, one of my spirit guides, gave me a lovely compliment. He said that many people talk about unconditional love, but that I have truly given it. He says that I have been a very good student, and I could teach him. Another spirit teacher, my Indian guide Manachuk, complimented me as well. He said that in this world nothing is given to us, we have to earn it. He had to earn the feathers on his headdress. He gave me spiritual feathers as a gift for the unconditional love I have given.

Love grows! The more love that you give, the more you attract. As you express your love, in whichever way you do it, your talents and ability to give to others will grow.

Love surrounds us. It is said that the Holy Spirit is in every breath that we take. It is called the sacred breath of life. Try not breathing. You can't do it for long. It only takes a simple request for God's love to be in your heart. Ask God for His love in your heart and soul. Then your soul's transformation will begin.

In Betty Eadie's book <u>Embraced by the Light</u>, she tells of her near-death experience. She learned that every blade of grass, every flower, every molecule in every rock and inanimate object is aware of love and of its creator, in different ways. The flowers are praising God as they lift their petals and create their brave beauty, as they thrust forth into the world blind, and yet trusting. Poets and writers and artists have expressed love in many ways throughout time. Some years back, people joined hands in an expression of love that crossed our nation as they joined together in a spirit of giving, and the following song was their theme:

> There comes a time when we heed a certain call,
> When the world must come together as one.
> There are people dying and it's time to lend a hand to life,
> The greatest gift of all.
> We can't go on pretending day by day that someone,
> Somewhere will soon make a change. We are all part of god's great big family and the truth
> You know, love is all we need.
>
> We are the world, we are the children, We are the ones to make a brighter day, So let's start giving. There's a choice we're making,
> We're saving our own lives, it's true,
> We make better days, just you and me.

Gentle Reparenting   The ORIGINAL Guide   J. Alvin

Bibliography and Resources:

We Are the World

Eadie, Betty J., <u>Embraced by the Light</u>, c. 1992, Gold Leaf Press

Harlow, Harry F., <u>Learning to Love</u>, c. 1971, Albion Publishing Company
Kirkwood, Annie, <u>Mary's Message to the World</u>, c. 1991, Blue Dolphin Press, Grass Valley, California

Moore, Thomas, <u>Care of the Soul</u>, c. 1992, HarperCollins Publishers, Inc.

Padgett, James E., <u>The Gospel Revealed Anew by Jesus</u>, first published 1941, by Foundation Church of the New Birth, P.O.Box 996, Benjamin Franklin Station, Washington, D.C. 20044

Sujata, <u>Beginning to See</u>, c. 1987 by Stillpoint Institute, Celestial Arts, P.O. Box 7327, Berkeley, CA 94707

Chapter 11

Epilogue

Our Native Roots

We live in an industrialized, technological culture in the USA. We have lost touch with our roots. We need to make peace with the part of our culture that separated our mind from our bodies and nature.

This separation happened generations ago, and the missing building blocks within most of the population that caused this breach with our whole selves was passed on to succeeding generations. We need to reclaim our ancient heritage, lost for so long.

This breach of our whole selves occurred as the survivors of famine and oppression fled Europe. They passed their unhealed traumas on to their children.

It occurred as people were snatched from villages in Africa, suffered horrors on slave ships, then led lives of misery and servitude. Their unhealed traumas were passed on to new generations.

This breach befell the American Indians, as their differences were belittled by the overwhelming numbers of newcomers to the land instead of being honored. Many Indian cultures were highly spiritual. There is no violence in the Hopi culture.

We need to make peace with and honor the wise people who occupied our lands so lovingly before the industrialized, "civilized" people came. These old ones were in harmony with the earth.

We need to make peace with races other than our own. Our separateness does both ourselves and the world great harm. Our partnership can offer us the treasures that each race, each nation, each people, each tribe, each person uniquely and beautifully has to share and teach, to heal and empower others.

Once we all lived in tribes. Prior to the nuclear family, before large extended families, before the technological revolution, before agriculture was developed and we settled into cities, we all lived in tribes. We all were close to the earth, and in close communion with our tribal others. We had a wisdom then of the earth and of our natures, that we lost degree by degree as we climbed the path to civilization as we express it in our lives today. We can shed those barriers that separate us from our source, of who we really are. We can discover and love the awesome, unique person that is in our core. We can discover who we really are.

The possibility exists that the indigenous people, the people who still remain, who have escaped '
"civilization," can be our teachers. They may still have what we "civilized" peoples lost five hundred or so generations ago.

Gentle Reparenting   The ORIGINAL Guide   J. Alvin

I use the term "civilized" in quotes, as we "civilized" peoples have developed and used sophisticated weapons to kill our fellow man. We dishonor the animal life in our care with factory farms and inhumane ways of killing. We kill the soil that nourishes us with chemicals. We have much to re-learn about honoring the earth, from whose bounty we receive everything we put in our mouths, and every man-made object that exists.

We may become able to become partners with all mankind. We may become better caretakers of the animal and plant kingdom, and of the earth itself. We may, through the lessons we learn, be able to connect with our whole selves. The future of life on our planet depends on our doing so.

We can develop the attitude that each person that crosses our path can teach us a beautiful lesson. Perhaps the lesson is as simple as, "I don't want that lesson, thank you."

We can expand this idea even further, and see that all life forms can teach us lessons. What lessons are offered by our pets? By the wildlife, by pests? What lessons are offered by our plants, by nature? What lesson is there in a sunset, a sunrise, the storms? What can we learn from the calm times? What about the disasters? Doesn't the best in us shine forth after disasters, as we help our fellow man?

Do we need disasters to bring out the best in us? Or can we look for that goodness within each of us in the calm times? Can we each look within and see what we can contribute to our fellow man, to the plants or animals, to the planet?

Dare To Dream

I have been so rewarded by the gifts of growth, love and understanding in the many therapies, educational experiences and personal growth courses I have taken. It always seems odd to me that people hear about these opportunities and turn them down. They spend hundreds of thousands of dollars on a home, a new car and beautiful wardrobes, and on other material things.

Then they look at the cost and time required for these courses, from free to $15 to $1,000. They are skeptical. They say no. They won't risk this relatively minuscule amount of their money and time. They won't take a chance to see if personal growth might be of value to them.

They won't listen to their friends who are <u>so</u> excited and want to share their experiences. Their friends see possibilities for them, but they won't listen. They won't look. Perhaps they are too resigned to the rut they are in. Maybe they are too hopeless to even look or dream anymore. Or maybe they are healthy and happy, and it does not occur to them to dream for more.

Did you look back over your accomplishments as last year drew to a close? What dreams did you have for the coming year? Did you make New Years resolutions?

Do you allow yourself to dream of a better tomorrow? What is your dream? Is it to have a loving relationship with someone, or perhaps a career change? Is it increasing your income? Has travel to an exotic country been one of your dreams? Maybe your dream is simple. Perhaps you want to see friends or relatives whom you haven't seen in a long time. And how many times have you told yourself, "Someday I am going to travel, find a partner, start my own business, buy a house, etc." The time is now. Are you resigned to the way things have been?

If you are resigned to the way things have been, you've buried your inborn imagination and enthusiasm. Only you can dig them out! The first step of reaching goals may be the hardest for you, as you dare to dream of the future that you want and know deep down that you deserve.

The next step after dreaming is to write down your dreams. Write your goals for ten years, five years, one year, and one month.

Then, picture yourself in the future, a success in fulfilling your dream. Now, from that point in the future, look back and outline the steps you took to succeed.

Is success in relationships your dream? Do you notice as you look back that your relationships are not what you want? Do you notice that they all have one thing in common? You were there in all of them! It may be time for personal growth or therapy. You deserve to spend your money on yourself. You are worth the investment.

Many thousands of people have given themselves the gift of spending their hard earned money on themselves by getting themselves in therapy or by pursuing personal growth courses.

Dare to take a calculated risk! Chances are you will find that the only thing to fear is fear itself. Or the only thing to be skeptical about is your own skepticism.

It has been said that the only difference between fear and excitement is remembering to breathe! Go for it! Take some action for yourself now!

New Horizons

Here's my vision and commitment on the far horizon. Peace is spreading across cities and nations. We can see it in the effort of all the major powers who averted a large war in the Middle East. Cooperation stopped Saadam Hussein's war machine in a few days. We can see peace expanding in many ways if we look. We are slowly moving in the right direction.

My commitment is that this type of healing becomes widely available, and makes a difference in many lives, and finally, in our culture.

I visualize a grass roots awareness of the deserving child within all of us. I dream of an awakening across the land. I see people acknowledging their own voids within. I see them judging others less harshly, aware that they are doing the best they can with the building blocks they have.

I dream of a grass roots request across the land for adults to have these early needs filled. I see these needs becoming open and honored, rather than hidden with shame.

I imagine pre-schools opening at night and on weekends. I see pre school teachers offering pre-school experiences to adults. I see elementary schools, junior high and high schools being aided by large numbers of volunteers who want to contribute to our children, our future.

I visualize churches and temples offering this type of healing, as they open to new expressions of unconditional love. I see them extending this unconditional love to other spiritual organizations than their own, honoring what the other people hold as sacred. I see the churches respecting the differences and beauty of other faiths. I see criticism and judgement fading, as the ability to honor and appreciate other viewpoints grows.

I dream that these loving, void-filling experiences will be available to all, as a birthright. I dream that every person with some building blocks of love will in some way help others. I visualize people offering these building blocks of love in every day places.

I dream of churches and temples reaching out to God's children, feeding and sheltering them.

I dream of seeing present day missionaries going in groups to paint, clean and repair the homes of our elders, our disabled, and our poor. I dream of seeing them giving their assistance unconditionally.

I dream of seeing hatred and fear being overcome by love. I dream of seeing TV, radio shows and movies reflecting the love and peace that is growing.

I see a blossoming of spiritual growth, the end result of emotional growth. I see devotional singing groups springing up in homes across the country.

I see the jails decline in numbers, as the inmates receive love and education, healing and support. I see the bars on the windows of peoples' homes coming off, as people feel safer and safer. I see true freedom returning to our land, as we all remove the bars in our minds.

I envision our elders being honored for their unique contributions and wisdom. I see intermingling of the generations, as people begin to appreciate all of the other ages and stages of life.

I envision people honoring Mother Earth. I see them adopting the Native American ways of asking permission of the earth and the creatures, and blessing the earth, before digging and bulldozing. I see growing numbers of open hearted people now unable and unwilling to pollute and raze the earth.

I dream of seeing the growth of loving groups, easing the loneliness and separateness of our people. I see the numbers of people who feel loved growing, until those who feel unloved are surrounded by love. I see cold hearts finally melting with love.   I dream of great numbers of people healing, all across the land. I see them reaching out into the pockets of despair. I see people packing an extra lunch as they make their own, to have something nourishing to give to their homeless and poor fellow humans.

I dream of the pockets of despair shrinking, as more and more people develop their capacity to give and share. The homeless, the poor, the teenagers, our elders, the immigrants will be touched by love and caring from all sides.

I believe that there is a seed of God planted within each one of us. Let's allow that seed to grow.

I envision the famine of the heart ebbing, and then ceasing to flow. It will start with you. Will you do your part to heal and to give? Your gifts are needed. Your love is needed.

God bless and guide you.

Love,

Jeannie

P.S. I believe in Magic (love)

Appendix

These are excerpts from the journal I kept as I began to heal in my sessions with Sam. You can travel with me on my journey.

All of my emotions and the feeling of hunger in my body were totally blocked. I felt pressure and discomfort, but did not actually feel my emotions, although I called the pressures I felt "panic," or other names of emotions. I called feeling less pressure "feeling good." More pressure and a headache meant "starving" to me. I had no energy, and always felt exhausted, because all of my energy was used to block my emotions.

I had never trusted another human. Most people rejected me very quickly, from friends to therapists.

In these notes I show the process of my coming alive. I began to feel all of my emotions, including love, and learned to trust others, starting with Sam.

I was an analytical person, a former computer programmer. I lived in my mind. In these pages you will see how the adult slipped into the background and my inner child, never allowed expression since my infancy, began to grow and learn and thrive.

The beginning of my regression to a childhood state is illuminated in these diary-like notes. Finally having some infant and childhood experienced is what gave me the health and the good life I enjoy today.

"COMING ALIVE," My Journal

from pages 10,11
March 31, 1980

When I felt the first weird sensations, they felt good. I asked Sam what that was, and he said, "It's called coming alive."

So I went to him each week and did a little breathing and my body shook and trembled, and I just noticed and thought it was interesting.

Then one day I was talking to my friend Mike and he said some mean things to me, and I started shaking like I did in my sessions with Sam. I asked Mike to account for what he said and told him I was shaking, and we did get it cleared up. Mike became very nurturing and said he was sorry he scared me.

Sam had said not to do the breathing exercises at home, which I was tempted to do because I liked the sensations. (Sam said the breathing exercises are called Reichian bodywork.) When I started shaking on the phone with Mike I thought I had accidentally done something wrong, maybe without realizing it I had done the breathing exercises when I was busy talking.

So I called Sam in a panic and told him that when I was talking with Mike the shaking started, and what should I do? Sam said that it was okay and don't worry about it, feelings would start coming up in between sessions.

It took about twenty-four hours of making connections, of remembering how I shook, and

Mike saying he was sorry he scared me, and Sam saying it was a feeling, for me to realize that I had felt scared. I never knew what feeling scared felt like, and now I do.   That was the beginning of me feeling and knowing it. The next week sadness came up. I felt sad talking to my friend and got tears in my eyes for about one second.

Then a few days ago I woke up at 4 a.m. with a strange sharp feeling in my stomach and ran to the kitchen and got milk. I'm pretty sure that was hunger. (Usually I feel pressure in my head or shake or lose energy, and that's when I know to eat. I've always called that being hungry, or starved, and didn't know that other people felt different when they said they were hungry.)

page 12
April 1, 1980
I'm going to ask Sam to show me what he does and says and looks like and acts like when he's angry. I don't want him to be angry at me, I just want to see him angry. I'll ask him to pretend there is someone there he is angry with and show me what he does.

pages 14,15
I called Sam last night at 7:30 p.m. I told him I was scared of being very angry at him, scared of his anger, and scared of abusing my son. He said to come over right then, so I did. We talked about my son and about keeping him in day care, and what I've done about finding a safe place for him. My

son was with a friend for the night. I feel great relief that he's safe and great relief that I don't have to worry about control.

I told Sam that I wanted him to give me baby bottles, and that there was a possibility of a bond forming between us, which I would then break as I moved through the developmental stages. I asked him to enter that dependency relationship, instead of remaining aloof, which is what most therapists do.

Sam asked me what that would mean in terms of time and ideal situations. I was unable to answer thinking of him in that position, I was too scared and sad thinking of how much I need and how likely it is that I won't get it.

Finally I told him what my ideal fantasy would be with someone, not him. I said that my son and I would live with that person, and I wouldn't have to be in charge of meals, and I would be in charge of my son's pre-school and babysitters, and I would get a baby bottle in the morning and at night, and talk over my day in the evening, so I'd know someone was there for me. He asked how long it might take, and my best guess was five years.

Sam said he was going to consider what I asked and give me an answer at another time. He had an unusual expression on his face, and his whole body. Sam's whole body seems to express feelings. His whole body expressiveness had an incredible impact on me.

Gentle Reparenting   The ORIGINAL Guide   J. Alvin

Then Sam said that someone who had been scheduled for the time when he was seeing me was waiting in his house, and asked if I thought fifteen or twenty minutes was enough for a bottle. I didn't know. I asked if I could wait until after his other appointment and Sam said no, that wouldn't work. So he said, "Let's give it a try."

So he went and heated the milk and came back. (I had brought a bottle and milk with me to show him.)

Sam sat back against the wall and I laid down in his arms and he held me. I felt surrounded by warmth and felt so good. He's so safe for me. I felt comforted all the way deep down into my tummy.

When I was done drinking, Sam held me still. Later he touched me and I got up. Sam asked me how I was doing, and I told him that I felt good.

Then I asked how he felt. Sam said he felt unusual. He'd never done that before. I asked him if it seemed weird. He said no. He seemed to be moving slowly and I felt comforted.

I asked Sam if I seemed young when he was feeding me, and he said yes. Again he had the most unusual, expressive look that I've never seen before all over his face and body.

page 21
9 a.m. April 4, 1980

Last night I lay down to go to sleep early and had a fantasy that I was over at Sam's talking to him and I got angry for about a second in front of him and he saw it. I made an angry face at him. I don't remember what I was angry about now.

Then I lay there awhile longer and felt good, from the inside of me to the outside. It just lasted a short time.

That's the first time that came from the inside of me, the only other time I felt it was when it came from Sam the two times when he held me.

I'm surprised that it could happen so quickly, and I think it's not supposed to. I think it's from doing the breathing the other night. I'm glad, though, because my body feels comfortable again and I'm not feeling the pressure I was feeling.

I woke up this morning and <u>ran</u> to the bathroom, <u>ran</u> back, took a bike ride, and went to do a million things. I have some energy! I'm pretty sure it's connected to feeling angry (if that's what I really felt, maybe this is just wishful thinking) for that one second. If I'm not holding my anger so tight I have some of my energy!

page 24

I got home from camp (an overnight with a friend) in a panic, and I couldn't figure out why I was scared. I called my friend Mike, and he suggested that I take a hot bath. I did. My tummy relaxed and came out a couple of inches.

Then I called Mike again and talked. I realized that my fear right now is fear of being punished for having feelings.

This fear came up as soon as the fear of being <u>immediately</u> rejected by Sam got calmed down by the phone call yesterday. Although I still think he'll reject me sooner or later.

page 28
3 a.m.   April 6, 1980

Sam will love me <u>no</u> matter what I do. An acquaintance, Sandy, says to say this five times an hour. She came up with that statement. After I told her how much I was convinced that Sam would reject me Sandy said to say that. She calls it an affirmation.

At first I couldn't even say it, then I whispered it. Then I said I'm willing to do hard things if it will help me.

Sandy said that Sam loves me in the greater scheme of things because he's my therapist. I know he doesn't. I'm just one of many clients. And probably the most unpleasant and bothersome of all.

page 29
April 8, 1980

I think I am starting to feel anger, hunger, and good in one-second long happenings every so often. I didn't think about feeling good, and wasn't looking for it as a lost emotion.

I thought lack of pain was how people felt when they felt good. I didn't know about this warmth from my inside.

And this morning I felt a little something, like a little cramp in my stomach when I was drinking my bottle. I think that was hunger. I think that is what other people feel instead of their head hurting.

page 32
5:45 a.m.   April 9, 1980
Sam called me Monday to tell me our appointment is going to be on Thursday. That's tomorrow. I'm still scared that he is going to reject me.

The level of fear is way down from last week, that was panic. As soon as I see Sam I am going to ask him if he has any thoughts of rejecting me.

Sam amazes me by knowing how to say just what I need to hear, or doing just what I need him to do. I know I'm going to get well, otherwise I wouldn't have found someone good for me. He's so good for me, and the only safe person I've ever found in the whole world.

page 39
6 a.m. April 10, 1980
I just got up from a nap. After seeing Sam my eyes were so sleepy I had to lic down. I feel so peaceful and quiet inside. I told him how I'm feeling the things I'm feeling, and about my son, and about my friends.

Then we talked about what we'd do together. Sam said we'd continue to meet three times a month for fifty minutes, and sometimes we could talk like we have been, and sometimes we'd do direct emotional work, and sometimes breathing exercises, and sometimes get bottles.

I said I want a bottle every time, and to do it until my mouth relaxed. Sam said okay, and went and heated my bottle.

I laid down on his chest and he held me. He smelled good and felt warm. It just takes a minute and then pressure builds in my head and I make a noise that probably sounds very sick. Then he feeds me my bottle.   It feels so good in my mouth. I'm aware of a certain pressure that Sam puts on the bottle and that feels good to me. I felt a little bit of a falling sensation and heard stomach noises, I couldn't tell if they were from inside or outside me. Then I felt like I was being rocked, like in a sailboat, as Sam would breathe and I'd go up and down. My mouth relaxed after I felt good awhile.

When Sam said it was time to grow up and be big again I stayed there for a minute and looked at Sam's eyes. I experienced it as looking in his direction, not as actually seeing him.

I think that is a big step for me. Before Sam gave me bottles I liked to look at his eyes, but the other times he gave me the bottle my eyes were shut tight. I couldn't look at him until I got away from him.

Driving home, my mouth felt very different from before, and looked different in my mirror. The good feeling is still there, and I don't want to be around anyone so I can keep this feeling as long as possible.

page 43

5:45 p.m.   April 11, 1980

I stopped being suicidal last year in Mexico. I was thirty-two years old, miserable, and lonely and starved for love as always, and I realized that I had made it a long time that way, I managed to make it through the long days and the long long nights. If I had made it that long, I could make it the rest of the way to whatever age I live to be.

One of the things that helped me survive my childhood were occasional kind acts, like when I was seven and a friend of my father's gave me a stuffed dog. I called him Doggie, and always slept with him and he became alive and loved me and never hurt me. I didn't realize he wasn't alive and I had made him that way with my imagination until I was in my first therapy about six years ago. I still feel comforted from stuffed animals and have been sleeping with my son's Teddybear recently.

page 50

I asked Sam if I were his worst client and a horrible bother. He said no. I asked if he thought I could get well with him. He said yes. I laughed and said I thought so too. I asked if he cared about me. He said yes.

page 59

6 a.m. April 14, 1980

I knew I have always taken things literally, which means I don't understand most jokes, and don't have much of a sense of humor. I didn't know that I would take everything Sam says as an order. Now that I know that, I can ask for what I need to hear, like I did this morning.

Now I'm comfortably and efficiently doing my chores, and thinking again. Being bound by Sam's words happens because I need so much from him, and have hope of getting my needs met, so everything Sam says is so important to me, more important than what anyone else could say. The only way I can possibly get my eighteen years of unmet childhood needs met is to get something important for me from everything Sam says and does and feels.

page 70

I need to ask for permission to feel. This taking things literally thing seems to be accelerating. Since Sam told me to do things, and hasn't told me to feel my feelings, I'm not feeling anything.

I think the reason it is accelerating is because I believed Sam the other day when he said he could help me get well and I agree, and I now trust him more than I've ever trusted anyone before.

I have given him all of my power, something I've never done ever before, and so he is all-powerful for me. I won't stop seeing him by my choice from now 'til I get well.

Gentle Reparenting   The ORIGINAL Guide   J. Alvin

I still expect him to reject me, but the point where I was capable of rejecting him is past. I am having my first thoughts of the possibility that he won't reject me. I can't imagine how I'd feel.

page 75,76

I forgot to write the most important thing. Sam said I sounded angry on the phone. I said, "Oh, maybe I am." I wasn't aware of any special physical response to put with it, but I do remember taking a breath before I said whatever it was that sounded angry. And that's all that happened.

We just went on talking about other things. Nobody got hurt, I didn't get scared. How can it be that something I've been so terrified of can be so small and quiet?

And my fantasies about Sam's reaction to my anger were full of drama, and loud and scary. All Sam did was comment.

All I think about it at this point is- -hmm. I'm a little disappointed that I am having so little reaction to finding a lost emotion and daring to express it to Sam, even though I didn't know what I was feeling. Maybe it's because I'm so sleepy my eyes won't stay open.

Today I got up at 4:30 a.m. for my morning bottle. This makes me laugh.

Tomorrow I see Sam! Hurray! I'm going to be so happy to see him. This is a new thing-- -laughing.

250

page 80

Getting Well -that's the name of this part

That list will have to wait until later. I ate and I put my Christmas record on to play over and over, <u>The Chipmunk Song</u>, and I'm going to the beach. Grocery shopping will have to wait. I want to go play. Goodbye book.

I had some vanilla ice cream left from Mike's birthday, so I made oatmeal for breakfast and put the ice cream on it. It was really good.

page 85
April 8, 1980

Questions for Sam, and an important thing to tell him:
1.	Do you have any thoughts in your mind about terminating me as your client?
2.	Is it okay for me to begin an exercise program?
3.	Can I have a bottle at the beginning so I can stop when I'm done and still be held some, instead of having to stop because you need me to?
4.	I would take your seeing me less than we are now as a rejection and as punishment for feeling my feelings. *******
5.	I felt four new feelings this week. ******
	energy
	hunger

anger

good

6.   What did you feel in response to my asking you about commitment and working too hard?

7.   I want a picture of Sam feeling.

252

Jeannie Alvin's books are available at

www.lulu.com/spotlight/awakening

www.lulu.com/spotlight/NewDiscoveries

www.amazon.com/-/e/B0755K7MHP

Awaken to Life! Better Than You Ever
    Dreamed!_8 games to play in the now

Change Games 2 of the games that change
    your life

Awakening To Our Oneness, Reflections after self
realization, poetic musings

Heart to Mind Healing, Power Affirmations to
Create a Healthy Ego with illustrations by artist
Suzanne Cerny

Going to Amma and Kalki? the 21 day course?
Amma's ashram, Nemam? practical preparation
information to go to Oneness University, plus a
history of the early days of Oneness Blessings.

Jeannie offers deeksha workshops based on her
discoveries for groups and organizations.